THE EYE OF A NEEDLE

FELDHEIM PUBLISHERS Jerusalem / New York

THE EYE OF A NEEDLE

AISH HATORAH'S KIRUV PRIMER

COMPILED BY
YITZCHAK COOPERSMITH

ISBN 0-87306-640-5 hardcover
ISBN 0-87306-641-3 paperback

Copyright © 1993
by Aish HaTorah

Feldheim Publishers
POB 35002/ Jerusalem, Israel

Feldheim Publishers
200 Airport Executive Park
Spring Valley, NY 10977

Printed in Israel

Dedicated to
the memory of
Rabbi Zecharya Graineman, ztz'l,

a father and brother
to so many of us.

Dedicated to
the memory of
my brother-in-law
Heshi Berger, ztz'l,

a true Oheiv Yisrael

בס"ד

23 Cheshvan 5753

The bnei Torah of our generation have perhaps a greater responsibility to get involved in *kiruv* than ever before. It has been amply proven that even the most assimilated Jew can be reached if properly approached, and it is therefore incumbent upon every one of us to take advantage of the unique opportunities presented by our *dor*.

Aish HaTorah has been a trailblazer in *kiruv*. Because of its extraordinary ability to present Torah in a contemporary, intellectually satisfying manner, tens of thousands of Jews have already been awakened to the beauty and relevance of Yiddishkeit. But there are countless more who are inaccessible to so limited an army of teachers. Every Jew who appreciates Torah must therefore take up arms and join the battle. In the words of Chazal, **Lo alecha hamlacha ligmor, v'lo ata ben chorin l'hibatel mimena...."**

Aish HaTorah has already cut a clearing for us in the thick forest of assimilation and apathy. Now we are fortunate to have the benefit of their insights and experience to enable us to widen the path. The Eye of a Needle can give the reader many essential tools and insights to become a "kiruv paramedic," and at the same time enrich his own appreciation and gratitude to the *Ribbono Shel Olam* for the great treasure that is Torah.

Rabbi Yaakov Weinberg
Rosh Yeshiva

דוד קאהן

ביהמ"ד גבול יעבץ
ברוקלין, נוא יארק

Rosh Chodesh Kislev 5753

I have read Aish HaTorah's Kiruv manual <u>The Eye of a Needle</u> and have found it to be an original, inspiring work that will be a valuable asset to those wishing to perform the important mitzvah of Kiruv Rechokim.

The book is based on Aish HaTorah's years of successful experience in outreach, guided by the outstanding wisdom and leadership of Rabbi Noach Weinberg, shlita. It is filled with insightful approaches to introducing secular Jews to Torah and to conveying the meaning and relevance of Yiddishkeit in a contemporary and intellectual fashion.

<u>Eye of the Needle</u> will not only help the layperson feel more comfortable dealing with nonobservant Jews, it will immeasureably enhance the reader's own appreciation of Torah.

דוד כ"ץ הנ"ל יצו שליט

ב״ה

OFFICE OF
THE CHIEF RABBI

Adler House Tavistock Square London WC1II 9IIN
Telephone: 071-387 1066 Fax: 071-383 4920

"THE EYE OF THE NEEDLE"

Haskama by the Chief Rabbi Dr Jonathan Sacks

We live in remarkable times. A new generation of Jewish youth
is searching for its identity, seeking its historical moorings
and looking for traditional values of a permanent nature. The
Teshuva movement in Israel, and indeed throughout the world,
is no longer a novelty. Every searcher needs a personal
guide, able to speak their heart in a challenging yet
welcoming and encouraging way.   Every guide needs a method
which will provide them with ideas and help them in the
provision of answers for those who are seeking.

"The Eye of the Needle" is a fascinating, most welcome and
much to be commended primer whose avowed task is to deal with
just this need.   It is a manual for all those who can and want
to help those far away discover and appreciate the truths of
Judaism.   It deals effectively and perceptively with many of
the seeming conflicts of Torah and science, Torah and
philosophy and Torah and contemporary social problems.

It is with the greatest pleasure that I recommend this book to
all those involved with outreach work and indeed, to all
readers searching for an intelligent interpretation of
Judaism.   The method and the suggested solutions in the book
reflect the style and approach of Aish HaTorah, its producers,
one of the most successful outreach organisations of our day.
One cannot help but be inspired and enlightened, guided and
informed by this illuminating presentation.

חדש ימינו כקדם

CONTENTS

How to Teach

Appendix

PREFACE

Aish HaTorah recently conducted a course on developing confidence and techniques for effective outreach for a group of concerned women in Brooklyn, New York.

In response to the many requests for transcripts and tapes of the material, we decided to put the contents of the program on paper. This book is in no way an exhaustive presentation of all the issues and approaches relevant to outreach. What follows is a crash course on some of the basic information a person needs to feel confident about teaching Judaism, as well as various approaches in outreach that we have found effective.

This handbook is only a beginning. We hope to crystallize more lessons from our experiences so that others can avoid the mistakes we made in learning how to reach out, and at the same time share and build upon our successes and breakthroughs.

In the eighteen years since the founding of Aish HaTorah, we have learned many lessons about successful outreach. The ideas and suggestions of many talented people have contributed greatly to this book. However, all of our efforts are built upon the extraordinary wisdom and insights of Rabbi Noah Weinberg, the founder and driving force behind Aish HaTorah and a foremost pioneer of the worldwide outreach movement. There is no page of this document that has not been influenced by his genius; only the writers should be held accountable for any flaw or lack of clarity in articulating these ideas.

I thank the following people for either writing or providing the framework for various sections of the book:

Rabbi Motty Berger: *The Historical Argument and the Psychology of Control Argument;* Rabbi Nachum Braverman: *Evolution;* Rabbi Avraham Mensch: *Critique of the Theory of Evolution;* Rabbi Yerachmiel Milstein: *The Gift of Life;* Rabbi Asher Resnick: *Tuma and Tahara, and Introduction to the Historical Argument. Jewish Women in Jewish Law* by Rabbi Moshe Meiselman and *The Invaluable Pearl* by Dr. Y. Ghatan provided some of the material for the section on Women in Judaism.

In particular, I would like to thank two people whose writing and editing skills improved this book enormously: Rabbi Yossi Glatstein and Aviva Edinger. (You the reader would thank them too, had you seen this book in its original form!)

Finally, I thank the following people for their contributions: Rabbi Dovid Cohen, Rabbi Eli Gewirtz, Rabbi Yitz Greenman, Rabbi Mordechai Haller, Mrs. Tzipporah Heller, Rabbi Ari Kahn, Mrs. Gila Manolson, Rabbi Yaakov Salomon and Rabbi Raphael Shore.

The publication of this book was made possible through the generosity of Pat and James Cayne and Beverly and Dick Horowitz.

Acharon, acharon chaviv. I would like to acknowledge with great appreciation the tremendous mesiras nefesh, always with a smile, by my wife, Bruchie. Thank you!

We are very interested in your feedback, questions or comments and will be happy to respond to any written inquiries.

Rabbi Yitzchok Coopersmith

FOREWORD

Chazal tell us that when God was prepared to give His Torah, He offered it first to the nations of the world.

"What is written in Your Torah?" inquired the nations.

"You shall not kill." "You shall not steal." "You shall not commit adultery," answered God.

One by one, each nation turned the Torah down. Until God came to the Jews.

Using what instantly became the most acclaimed expression in its national lexicon, the Jewish people replied "*Na'aseh, V'Nishmah.*" "We will do, and we will listen." No information is necessary; if You are offering it, we will take it without question.

The Midrash continues with a baffling statement about God's reaction.

"*Mi gila raz zeh l'banai?*" asked God. "Who revealed to My children this secret expression, used only by my heavenly angels [to say 'we will do' before 'we will listen']?"

Was this a logical question for *God* to ask?

What was God thinking? Did He believe there was a high-level leak in His cabinet? Or that some careless angel let the cat out of the bag and told the Jews what to say?

Obviously, no one but God could have provided the Jews with information only the angels possessed. So what exactly was He asking?

Clearly, the Midrash is trying to teach us something much more profound about this episode.

In Parshas Yisro, we learn that before giving the Torah to the Jews, God instructed Moses: "Ko somar l'vais Yaakov v'sagid l'vnai Yisrael." "So shall you say (the verses below) to the house of Jacob and relate to the Children of Israel." Rashi explains, "You shall tell them *exactly* these words. No more, no less."

> 1. Chapter 19, Verse 4: "You saw what I did to the Egyptians. Egypt had been worshipping idols for years, but I didn't destroy them until they made you suffer. Then, I carried you on wings of eagles and brought you close to Me.
> 2. Chapter 19, Verse 5: "If you listen to My Torah, all will be good for you. You will be more precious to Me than all the nations. I created the entire universe and I will place it in your hands, for your enjoyment."
> 3. Chapter 19, Verse 6: "The Torah will turn you into a nation destined for greatness — Mamleches Kohanim V'Goy Kadosh. You will be a priestly nation, a nation of kings."

Why were these words so crucial? Because this was exactly the message the Jews needed to hear so that they would accept the Torah without reservation.

"I, God, created you out of My love for you. You have seen how I have cared for you and carried you close to Me. The entire world is Mine, and of all the nations, I have made you My most treasured. Now I am going to offer you a chance to enjoy greatness and glory beyond that of any people. I am going to give you the Torah."

How would you respond to such an offer?

Imagine that your father came to you with a deal. Before he presented it, he said, "Son, you know I love

you. Everything I've ever done for you is for your benefit. Now I've arranged a deal for you that will bring you
great happiness."

Would you expect the son to say, "Let's see, Dad.
Leave your proposal with me for a few days. I'll look it
over, decide if it's really worthwhile, and I'll get back to
you."

Of course not! The instinctive reaction would be:
"Fine! I'll take it!" For the son knows, through every
experience he's ever had, that if his father has something for him, it's for his benefit only. He won't need to
analyze the deal; he'll grab it.

This is why the Jews instinctively responded with,
"Na'Aseh V'Nishmah." They understood the most fundamental reality of Torah: It is a chance to seize the
gold ring. We are not doing God a favor by keeping
the mitzvos. To the contrary. God is giving us the
opportunity of a lifetime.

This is the message you must internalize and convey as you reach out to other Jews; this is your calling
card. Teach people that to do a mitzva is to invest in
yourself. Teach them that opportunity is knocking —
and that all they need do is open the door and start
down the path to greatness.

Rabbi Noah Weinberg
Dean
Aish HaTorah College of Jewish Studies

INTRODUCTION

Assimilation is ravaging our people. With a force more insidious and methodical than bullets or Scud missiles, this quiet killer is slowly unraveling the fabric of the Jewish nation.

Nowadays it is increasingly difficult to ignore the grave impact assimilation has had within North America and throughout every Jewish community in the diaspora. Articles carried in nearly all the major media predicting the potential disappearance of the vast majority of Jews in North America are shocking both Jews and non-Jews throughout the world.

Assimilation in North America is not a sudden, present day problem or an impending catastrophe. It has been an escalating problem for the last 150 years.

In 1888, of the 200 synagogues then in North America, *188* were Reform and incorporated close to two hundred thousand Jews.[1] Today it is virtually impossible to find any of these people's descendants in a synagogue. The vast majority have assimilated.

In little over 100 years, the offspring of those 200,000 Jews alone should have grown (even by conservative estimates) into over one million Jews. Instead, hardly a trace of these American Jewish pioneers remain, and a potent arsenal of the energy, creativity and strength of one million Jews is lost to us forever.

---

1. Encyclopedia Judaica, Vol. C.

The threat today is even greater. The Council of Jewish Federations in conjunction with the Mandel Berman Institute — North American Jewish Databank, recently released its findings from a comprehensive study of the Jewish population in North America. The study revealed a Jewish population of 5.5 million. Of that number, only 600,000 consider themselves to be Sabbath observers. An overwhelming 4.9 million Jews do not.

The problem does not stop there. According to the report, of all Jews who married within the last five years, 52% married a non-Jewish spouse. At this rate, of the one million unmarried Jews between the ages of 18 and 40, at least 450,000 will marry a nonJew over the next 10 to 15 years. After a person decides to intermarry, it is only a matter of time before they and their children disappear as Jews. As shown by the survey, only a small minority — 28% — of those raised in a mixed household were raised as Jews.

Assimilation is spinning out of control. Considering the impact that innovations such as patrilineal descent will have on the decisions Jews make about whom they marry, it appears nearly certain that this problem has not yet reached its peak.

What Can and Must Be Done

Intermarriage is not our main enemy. Ignorance is.

Jews who understand the value of Judaism make it a priority to marry a Jewish spouse.

Unfortunately, the vast majority of Jews in North America have not received the kind of Jewish education that fosters such commitment. Somehow, we must attract and educate these people — quickly, efficiently and effectively.

The challenge is daunting, but not insurmountable. As recent years have shown, the dedicated efforts of Jews who have committed their lives to educational outreach (kiruv) are already making headway. Creative programs displaying the treasures of wisdom and fulfillment that Judaism offers have awakened in thousands of Jews a new attraction to their heritage. It has been proven that we *can* reach even the most assimilated Jews.

While we would all like to believe that the problem of rampant assimilation is being fought effectively by kiruv professionals and that the tide is beginning to recede, this is unfortunately not the case. Although, baruch Hashem, many people have become Torah-observant Jews and many more have been developing in this direction, large numbers are still being lost to us every year.

What is needed is a method of attracting that segment of Jewry which has no interest in Judaism and bringing them to existing outreach programs. Servicing those who are eager to learn is relatively easy for experienced kiruv workers. The more difficult task is to stimulate interest in Jews who are completely alienated and apathetic.

Clearly, if we rely solely on full-time kiruv professionals, we will not have sufficient manpower and resources to combat the problem.

There is but one solution. The great, untapped resource of thousands of people who understand the necessity of kiruv and who come into daily contact with secular Jews. People who are in key positions to kindle the interest of secular Jews and invite them to attend an outreach program.

The Orthodox Jewish community of North America.

Each Orthodox Jew knows a secular Jewish person — a neighbor, relative or co-worker. If each Orthodox Jew were to recruit these people to a local outreach organization, or, better yet, become a para-outreach worker, we will have mobilized a grass-roots effort large enough to turn the tide back in our favor.

The obligations of a Jew to reach out to his alienated brethren are numerous and compelling.

The mitzvos of "Ve'ahavta l'rayacha kamocha," "Lo saamod al dam rayecha," "Hochayach tochiyach," and Kiddush Hashem all underscore the reality of "areivus" — the unity and co-responsibility of all Jews — and direct us to spare no effort in safeguarding the spiritual wellbeing of a fellow Jew.

This responsibility was forcefully articulated by Rav Moshe Feinstein, ztz'l, in an address that was reprinted in the Jewish Observer in June 1973. Rav Feinstein exhorted all Orthodox Jews, because of the precarious spiritual state of the Jewish nation, to "maaser" their time for outreach efforts. (See appendix for the complete article and a Kol Koreh signed by Rav Shach, shlita, the Steipler Gaon, ztz'l, and Rav Chaim Shmuelevitz, ztz'l.)

The Chofetz Chaim too, (in his famous work *Chomas Hadaas*, written in the early 1920's) emphasized the tremendous obligation upon us to reach out to unaffiliated Jews and the severity of neglecting this charge. If the Chofetz Chaim was admonishing people to do kiruv in the 1920's, how much more emphatic would he be today!

In the days of Joshua, the entire Jewish nation was held accountable for the mistake of one man. When Achan violated the prohibition against collecting the spoils of the battle of Jericho, the entire nation lost its Divine protection and suffered enormous casualties.

Why?

The Jewish people are one unit. The spiritual health of the body of Klal Yisrael is affected for good or bad by every member; therefore the destiny of each Jew is inextricably tied with the action of his neighbor. The level of the entire nation and the merit it has earned can come crashing down through the actions of a single person.

The Talmud (Shabbos 55a) recounts a fascinating exchange between God and the angels which teaches us a profound lesson about the depth of our mutual responsibility.

In Ezekiel 9:4, it is written: "God said (to the angel), go through the city — through Jerusalem — and make a mark on the foreheads of the people who sigh and cry for all the abominations that have been done there. Make a mark with ink on the foreheads of the righteous so that the angels of destruction should not attack them. Make a mark with blood on the foreheads of the wicked, so that they should be attacked by the angels of destruction."

The Attribute of Justice said before God, "Master of the Universe: How is one group different than the other?"

(God) replied, "One consists of the perfectly righteous, while the other consists of the absolutely wicked."

(The Atttribute of Justice) said, "Master of the Universe, they [the righteous] were able to protest and did not do so."

(God) said, "It is revealed and known to Me that even if they would have protested, it would have had no effect."

(The Attribute) replied, "If it is revealed to You, was it then revealed to them?"

It is thus written, "They [the Angels of destruction] began with the elders who were in front of the Temple."

Rav Yosef taught, "Even those people who kept the entire Torah from A to Z, perished because they did not correct the wicked."

This is the punishment given to a generation about whom God Himself testified could not have succeeded no matter what the effort. How great will be our shame if in our generation — when success is clearly within our grasp — we don't even make the effort!

We are one people with one destiny. Each of us is responsible for the actions of the other. A handful of people have already made a lasting impact on the face of the Jewish community in North America. If we join together, we will surely merit the power to bring back the entire Jewish nation.

Tools for Getting Started in Outreach

GAINING CONFIDENCE

One of Judaism's most famous converts was Onkeles, the son of a Roman Emperor, who left his home to study Judaism in Israel. The Talmud relates that the Emperor dispatched a battalion of solders to bring Onkeles back home and prevent him from converting. But after the soldiers reached Onkeles and engaged him in conversation about Judaism, all of them ended up converting too! The Roman Emperor sent a second battalion and again, all of them converted. Finally, in frustration and fury, the Emperor sent a third group of soldiers and commanded them to seize Onkeles and bring him back — while avoiding any conversation with him at all.

As they were taking hold of Onkeles, the soldiers saw him reach up and kiss a mezuzah. "What's that?" they asked. Onkeles replied . . . and, like the units before them, all these soldiers converted too. (The Emperor gave up after that, and Onkeles went on to become a great scholar in Israel.)[1]

What was the secret of Onkeles's extraordinary success? What did he say that was so compelling that in such a short amount of time he was able to convince the soldiers to change their lives?

Our rabbis tell us, "Devarim ha'yotzim min ha'lev nichnasim el ha'lev."[2] "Words that come from the heart, enter the heart." This was Onkeles' secret. Onkeles was

---

1. Bavli, Avoda Zara 11a
2. Sefer Shiras Yisrael, Rabbi Moshe Ibn Ezra, p. 156

so clear, so *real*, so absolutely convinced of the truth and beauty of Judaism, that the soldiers could not fail to absorb his conviction. Onkeles' responses were not merely words. They were alive with inspiration and meaning. Being in his presence was like experiencing a revelation. The power and energy Onkeles radiated as a result of the extraordinary level of spirituality and commitment he attained, is what struck the soldiers each time and moved them to embrace Judaism.

Herein lies the first key to success in outreach. In order to begin helping others understand why Judaism is meaningful and important, we must feel that way about it ourselves. Like Onkeles, we must be unshakeably convinced and enthusiastic about Judaism, because our own real-life example will be more persuasive than any logical argument. Morever, when we see someone start to vacillate during his search, or experience conflicts or pressures, our own confidence in Judaism will enable us to be an anchor that continuously reassures the person that the struggle is worthwhile.

At this point you may be wondering, "Why the emphasis on conviction? After all, I already appreciate the beauty and relevance of Judaism."

We live in a society whose values and goals are completely contrary to Jewish ones. We are subjected to a continuous barrage of information which has a powerful influence on how we perceive our Jewishness. No matter how strong or secure we are, we may occasionally feel that secular society does have some advantages over Judaism.

While most of us understand intellectually that Judaism is a better way of life, our ability to be effective in kiruv will be seriously hampered if these conscious or subconscious feelings of inferiority take hold on any level.

The following story illustrates just how pervasive society's influence is — an influence so subtle, many of us are not consciously aware of its persistent drain on our national pride and self-image.

In a program on Jewish self-awareness conducted by Aish HaTorah, a group of non-observant Jewish college students were asked to compile a list of traits they thought Jews possessed, positive and negative. The lists drawn up were largely negative: Jews were described as cheap, elitist, controlling the media, and other derogatory stereotypes.

Next the students were asked to prepare a list of things they associated with *Orthodox* Jews. These lists included even more outrageous and contemptible traits.

Finally, one long compilation of all the lists was drawn up and distributed.

The students were then shown a movie called "The Eternal Jew," one of the Nazis' chief propaganda tools to arouse the gentile population to participate in killing Jews. They were instructed to identify every point at which the movie portrayed a Jew in a negative light and describe how it was done.

After the film, the students compared the notes they had made of the film, with their personal lists about the Jews.

The two lists were shockingly similar.

Undoubtedly, the messages emitted by our society about Jews have penetrated our collective psyche. Although these messages are not trumpeted from the rooftops as they were in Nazi Germany, American society is transmitting many of the same signals — albeit in softer tones. And as strong as our personal convictions may be, we often cannot avoid succumbing to feelings of inferiority or self-doubt. Taking the time to understand and resolve these feelings will help maximize your effectiveness in outreach.

In conclusion:

Remember: clarity and enthusiasm are our most powerful tools. To be like "Onkeles," we must be convinced that Judaism is *gold* — and that this is a commodity every Jew needs.

And indeed it is. In explaining the numerous statements in biblical, prophetic and rabbinic literature comparing Torah to water,[3] our rabbis tell us that just as one cannot survive for more than three days without water, so too, a Jew can not subsist spiritually for more than three days without Torah.

This, incidentally, is why the rabbis instituted public Torah reading every Monday and Thursday. They wanted to insure that no Jewish community would be without Torah learning for more than three days at a time.[4]

Two caveats. First, believing that Torah Judaism is an infinitely superior ideology does not qualify one to judge *individuals* who are not observant. Always bear in mind that human beings can only judge *specific actions or opinions*, not people. A person who has no knowledge of Judaism could possibly be a better person in God's eyes than an observant Jew.

---

3. Tanna D'Bei Eliyahu Raba, 2:18 (among others)
4. Rambam, Hilchos Tefillah, 12:1

Second, while Judaism is undoubtedly superior to any other ideology, it is important to acknowledge the many worthwhile contributions to humanity made by people of other faiths, including technological advancements, religious and political freedoms, and medical and legal breakthroughs. While your focus should be on the overall benefits of Judaism, the contributions of other societies should never be discounted or denied.

What follows now is not necessarily information you will need to convey to a non-observant person. It is information that is primarily to bolster and refine your own appreciation of Judaism's uniqueness, so that the image you present will be as close as possible to Onkeles: secure, confident and keenly aware of the treasures that lie in Judaism.

The Four Universal Needs

There are four deep seated, psychological needs that every thinking being has: *meaning*, *pleasure*, *understanding* and *self-actualization*. For the Jew, these needs can only be met through the observance of a Torah lifestyle. Without Torah, the neshama (soul) lacks the essentials for lasting spiritual and emotional satisfaction, whether one is conscious of it or not.

1. *Meaning.*

> *"Man's search for meaning is the primary motivation in his life and not a 'secondary rationalization' of instinctual drives . . ."*
> *"A public-opinion poll was conducted a few years ago in France. The results showed that 89 percent*

of the people polled admitted that man needs 'something' for the sake of which to live."
—From *Man's Search For Meaning,* by internationally renowned psychiatrist Viktor E. Frankl

According to Western ideology, there is no absolute purpose to life. Good and evil, meaning and meaninglessness, are matters of personal taste. Yet with all the "freedoms" this philosophy embraces, it disposes of the one and only ingredient that gives life its potential for profound and lasting satisfaction: a transcendant purpose — the recognition of a Creator Who cares about man's actions and Who invests him with the ability to make choices that either further God's purpose or undermine it.

As vitally as he needs to breathe, eat and sleep, every human being needs to know that his existence matters. The philosophies of relativism and purposelessness, however, inevitably engender in man gnawing questions about the meaning and purpose of his life. "If nothing really matters, why am I making all these efforts to be a good person? Is life really about filling the time until my inevitable burial and decomposition?"

Understandably, this creates a subconscious anxiety which many people dread confronting directly. Better to be superficially convinced that life has no purpose at all, than to zero in on the tormenting realization that I have lived life in ignorance of that purpose.

Those who do confront the question, often embark on a painful, protracted search for meaning, frequently drifting through the array of alternatives to Western values, such as Zen, Buddhism and Transcendental Meditation. The greater majority, however, accept society's insistence that there are no answers, and try to deaden their pain through various mediums of distraction. Some lose themselves in the world of entertainment and illusion — television, movies, video games. Others dedicate mind and soul to "making it" in their careers. Many, in an attempt to relieve their anxiety, adopt the belief that there is no Creator, no responsibility, no accountability and no goals. Without a viable alternative to meaninglessness, these people have no choice but to avoid contemplating life too seriously.

But despite the best efforts of distraction and rationalization, their souls' longing for meaning cries out deep inside them. And until the soul receives the nourishment (read: meaning and purpose) it so vitally needs, man will never find lasting tranquility. On some level, (most often subconscious) he will continue to be plagued by the disharmony between what he deeply craves and what Western ideology claims life has to offer.

To illustrate, imagine you have started a new job. You show up Monday morning at 9:00 a.m., eager to begin work, prepared to receive a set of tasks and instructions. But, to your surprise, there is no manager on hand to tell you what your responsibilities are, what rules you are to follow, and how to use your time meaningfully. You want to contribute something meaningful, but you have no idea how to direct your energy and enthusiasm.

After sitting idly for a few days, you finally decide, "I might as well do something." So you look around and try to get an idea of what the operation is about.

You ask your co-workers, "How can I be helpful? What can I do that is of real value?" But they mock your earnestness and deride your enthusiasm as naivete. "There is no point," they tell you. "There is no rhyme or reason to our actions; there is no goal for us to attain."

You are shocked and confused. Your spirits are dampened. But you decide to press on still. When you spot different ways to be helpful, you pitch in and lend a hand. You do some things that in your assessment seem to be valuable contributions to the overall good of the company. But you are never quite sure if your efforts are worthwhile.

After doing this for a month, you learn that the company president will be coming in in three days to evaluate your work and decide if your time has been well spent or wasted. Your colleagues are stunned, and you feel extremely nervous. "How do I determine with confidence whether I did a good job or not? Am I going to be made to feel that I wasted my time here, or was I indeed productive and of benefit to the enterprise?

Anyone can appreciate how unsettled they would feel in that situation. And underneath it all, this is how many people feel when they reflect back on their lives to evaluate what they have accomplished.

"Ashreinu mah tov chelkeinu, u'mah naim goraleinu!" As Torah Jews, our inner longing to lead meaningful, productive lives is nurtured and guided from the start. In early childhood our parents and teachers outline the goals we are to strive for. We are given a clear set of instructions to help us accomplish those goals and measure our progress. The goal is our relationship with God, our tools are the mitzvos and the obstacles to avoid are the avairos. The framework for success and meaningfulness is neatly laid out for us in the intricate structure of Torah. Best of all, we need not struggle to find the goal. We are free to focus our energies and resources on achieving it.

Through Torah, the most mundane and routine activities of life are elevated. With the blessing "Asher Yatzar," even going to the bathroom becomes an opportunity to enhance our appreciation of God's greatness and our love for Him. And while we may never accomplish all that we should, a Torah lifestyle removes the specter of meaninglessness that haunts our nonobservant friends and neighbors. We have internal stability, gained from the knowledge that life is purposeful and valuable; and we are given ongoing opportunities to accomplish things that are unmistakeably meaningful. The realization that our choices truly matter is tremendously empowering and reassuring, and it rescues us from foundering helplessly in a sea of confusion and illusion.

2. *Lasting Pleasure.*

Western ideology tells us to live for pleasure: "If it feels good, do it."

Indeed, today more than ever, everything is permissible, and available in excess.

But are people significantly happier now than they were years ago?

It seems that while Western society has rendered everything permissible to us, what is available on the marketplace is obviously not enough to give people real fulfillment.

Look around. See how many members of our society seek escape. How many thousands of successful, talented people regularly lose themselves in drugs, alcohol, entertainment, sports, and the multitude of illusions designed to distract them from the reality of life. Calculate the exorbitant amounts of time and money spent in this country in pursuit of illusory pleasures: a bigger car, the next vacation, a fancier house.

But nothing satisfies the craving for lasting, meaningful pleasure.

Final Exit, a book on how to commit suicide in the comfort of your own home, appeared on the New York Times best seller list — a clear indication of how many people are not receiving the type of pleasure that makes the effort of living worthwhile.

To be fulfilled, a human being needs higher, more sublime pleasures than the experiences a physical world can provide. After all the money has been made, all the foods tasted, and all the honor and power achieved, there is still something missing, something which makes all other pleasures fade in comparison.

It's called *the transcendental*. The experience of a Presence infinitely greater than ourselves. An awareness of the reality and awesomeness of God.

Occasionally, people get a glimmer of this experience. Perhaps if they catch a sunset that takes their breath away with its splendor. Or witness the wondrous miracle of the birth of a baby.

That sensation, that experience of awe, is the feeling they get when their neshama senses its Creator. In their inner core, they know they have been in touch with something far grander than their five senses alone can grasp.

Ultimately, lasting pleasure of this kind is found only by tapping into the spiritual experiences of kedusha and ruchnius. These experiences are what make life continuously refreshing and energizing for the Jew. Through Torah and mitzvos, the Jew connects with the Ratzon Hashem and touches the transcendental on a daily basis, forging within himself a deeper and deeper connection to its Source. The Jew was *created* to receive this elevated pleasure. Without it, he will always be left wanting.

Consider how routine and flat your weeks would become if, for example, you didn't have Shabbos, the day set aside for the Jew to refine his appreciation of God's presence in the world. One day would run into the next and never leave you time to break out of life's mundane routine and experience the transcendental.

People who have no Shabbos, or any similar experience of kedusha, feel an emptiness in their lives — despite being "free" to partake in all the pleasures the world offers. Since the Western world has only a superficial understanding of pleasure, its merchandise can not satisfy on a deep level. People who invest more and more into the physical world will ultimately become less and less fulfilled.

Torah, on the other hand, offers access to the full range of pleasures, from the simple enjoyment of good food to the ecstasy of Ahavas Hashem,[5] the grandest of all pleasures.

3. *Tools for Living.*

Mankind's creative genius for harnessing technology to make life more comfortable has resulted in the proliferation of an enormous range of machines and

---

5. lit., "love of G-d"

gadgets. From the basic to the complex, almost every instrument comes with an "owner's manual," a set of instructions that enable the customer to derive optimum benefit from his purchase.

We can't program a VCR without first reading the instructions. Learning to fly a plane may take months of lessons. Performing brain surgery requires years of intensive study and training. The more complicated the procedure, the more we need preparatory training and detailed instructions.

While we all understand the need to spend years preparing for a career, few take the time and effort to properly equip themselves for life's most complex and potentially rewarding challenges: choosing a spouse, making a marriage work, raising well-adjusted children, actualizing one's potential, being a moral person, and building a flourishing society.

There is nothing inherent in Western life that imbues man with the clarity or focus to live life effectively. Nor are there any schools that address the challenges of living. The purpose of secular education is to learn how to make a living, not how to live.

Without a solid foundation in place, individual and communal life will not withstand well the tests of time. Left to his own devices and without the prerequisite tools for meeting these challenges, man is bound to confront obstacles which he is ill-equipped to surmount. The evidence is all around us. The rampant problems plaguing our society — divorce, drug abuse, depression, suicide, alcoholism, murder, rape, — speak loudly enough.

But while American society is critically ill at the youthful age of 200 plus years, the Torah lifestyle is still vibrant and flourishing more than 3,300 years after its inception.

The word "Torah" literally means instructions. Toras Chaim, as it is referred to in our prayerbook, means "instructions for living." From the time he begins to learn, the Torah Jew is immersed in a curriculum that provides him with the tools for successful living. With daily, weekly, monthly and annual mitzvos embracing the length and breadth of life, Judaism charts the way for us to develop our potential to the fullest.

When we step back and look at the wealth of practical and ideological lessons woven through the life cycle of a Jew and compare it with the life cycle of a secular person, the contrast is stark. Compare Rosh Hashana and its awesome significance with a New Year's Eve celebration in Times Square.

Whether it is interpersonal relationships, self-awareness, dealing with parents, choosing a spouse, building a cooperative community, animal rights or environmental concerns, Torah spans the gamut of human activity and is the ultimate "owner's manual" for maximum benefit from the world and from our lives. To ignore it is a tragedy.

Note: While Torah society is not entirely problem-free, most of the difficulties which do exist occur precisely when its members subordinate Torah values to that of the popular culture.

4. *Reaching Our Potential.*

Everyone wants to be great. As we grow older, however, and begin to understand how daunting and confusing a task it is, many of us settle for something less; the price of greatness is simply too high.

Yet we are all potential virtuosos at living; God implants within each of us the capacity for greatness. But when that potential is not brought to life, we experience frustration, just as a concert pianist who is denied the means to express his talent experiences frustration.

To attain any level of competence, however, we need more than just desire. We need clear guidance: a vision to strive for, and the tools with which to reach our vision.

The Torah is our instruction manual for greatness. It provides the framework that helps a person understand himself psychologically and spiritually. There are clear goals to aspire to, and practical observances and tools that help us reach our ideals. There are role models to emulate, who show us what is truly practical and attainable. The Torah way of life helps us tap into our potential and shepherds us along the road of becoming the people we want to be.

Western culture cannot focus on teaching values, because values are considered subjective and relative. Schools can teach reading, writing and arithmatic, but they are completely ineffectual in teaching students morals and ethics. Consequently, Western culture spawns generations of people who are frustrated at not being able to realize their potential, people who are confused about who they are and what direction their lives should take.

Conclusion

Imagine that you were never taught about the purpose of life. You had no concrete way of knowing if your life was good or if your existence mattered. Your time was spent acquiring material possessions; your spiritual side was all but ignored. You weren't sure if God existed, never mind experiencing His greatness and love for you. You cynically viewed the moral staples of Jewish life as outdated and naive: Kibud Av V'Aim, Shalom Bayis and Derech Eretz were not fashionable. You did not know the difference between the desires of your Yetzer Hara and the pull of your Yetzer HaTov. Take away the entire connection to reality and clarity that you have through Torah.

How would you feel? Off balance? Confused? At a loss as to how to attain the satisfaction and pleasure you know life should produce?

The more you can summon up that feeling, the better you can appreciate what Judaism offers, and the closer you will be to becoming an "Onkeles" in kiruv. Just being frum and doing mitzvos protects us from a lot of the world's nonsense and preserves our sense of self. Judaism gives us a basic working nourishment that no man-made ideology can supply.

Because, for so many of us, Torah observance is taken for granted, we may not easily recognize how lacking we would be without its insights, values and spirituality. Take a step back for a moment, though, and you will gain the perspective to truly appreciate the many benefits and advantages of Torah life. With this awareness, you will achieve the clarity and motivation to share your riches with others — in other words, to take on the challenges and joys of kiruv.

CLARIFYING
OUR OWN CONVICTIONS

People are sometimes intimidated by the idea of studying with a non-frum person. They worry about being asked questions they will not be able to answer, or giving answers that may be ineffective. They are concerned that some questions may reveal that they have accepted a concept without thinking it through.

Feeling unprepared to be a spokesman for Judaism is normal. Don't let it prevent you from getting involved. First of all, you know a lot more than you realize, and far more than most secular Jews. Second, your sincere desire to give of your time and friendship will go a long way to minimize the consequence of any gaps in your knowledge.

In truth, getting involved in outreach work will not only be beneficial for your students, but will ultimately be a very rewarding educational experience for you. Having to respond to all types of questions will motivate you to learn about those aspects of Judaism that you may never have thought about before.

Chazal tell us, in Pirkei Avos (Ethics of the Fathers), "Dah mah shetashuv l'apikores."[1] "Know how to respond to an Apikores." On the other hand, the

---

1. Actually, in our generation, no Jew can be called an Apikores. In order to warrant that title, one must have been given proper Tochacha and still persist in his ways. Since our generation is unable to give Tochacha correctly, no Jew can fall into

Rambam, in Hilchos Avodas Kochavim, states that it is forbidden to engage an Apikores in debate. How are we to resolve this discrepancy?

The answer is that we are encouraged to *know* how to answer an Apikores — not for his benefit, not to enter into debate with him — but for our own stability. If we do not learn the proper responses, the challenges posed by the Apikores will raise doubts and confusion in our minds. There is no neutral ground. Either we eliminate the confusion or the confusion will overwhelm us.

How do we rid ourselves of confusion? The first step is to determine which tenets and concepts we are confident of and which we are unsure about. This is not easy to do because it requires an intimate knowledge of ourselves and of our level of understanding. Therefore, to facilitate this process, we have prepared a list of questions touching on many essential ideas that every Jew should understand. This questionnaire is a good starting point to highlight those topics which require more information and clarity.

We can divide all of our convictions into one of four categories: knowledge, belief, faith and socialization. *For the purpose of this questionnaire only*, we have defined the categories as follows:

Knowledge is information you are absolutely confident of. For example, the fact that you have ten fingers.

Belief is a conviction for which you have some evidence, but lack complete proof. For example, you

---

the halachic category of Apikores. (See Chazon Ish, Yoreh Deah, Hilchos Shechita, end of Si'if 28.)

may believe that your regular customer's check won't bounce.

Faith denotes a desire to believe something, even though there is no evidence to support it. For example, a chain smoker may have "faith" that he will not succumb to lung cancer.

Socialization occurs when you accept something simply because society has conditioned you to believe it. For example, to be a successful person, you must go to college.

The first step is to ask yourself whether you think a particular conviction is true or false. Then specify in which of the four categories it lies. This will help you define those issues which need clarification.

Many of the issues raised in this questionnaire are dealt with throughout the remainder of this book, so do not be overly concerned that you will be raising questions for yourself that you will have problems answering.

CONVICTIONS LIST

Instructions: First circle True or False by each conviction. Then circle what level you believe (that it's true or false).

    A. Knowledge — like having five fingers, you're sure you're right
    B. Belief — you have evidence, but there's still room for doubt
    C. Society — has told you, but you have no evidence
    D. Faith — you desire it to be true, so you believe it

| 1. | The world is round. | TF | KBSF |
| 2. | Rich people are necessarily happier than poor people. | TF | KBSF |

3.	Going to college helps people understand what they want out of life.	TF	KBSF
4.	It is likely that most people's beliefs and ideas come from their societies.	TF	KBSF
5.	God does exist.	TF	KBSF
6.	Existence itself is proof that God loves us.	TF	KBSF
7.	The Oral Torah was also divinely given.	TF	KBSF
8.	The area of disagreement within the Talmud is relatively small.	TF	KBSF
9.	The world, as we know it, would still be pagan if not for the Jewish people.	TF	KBSF
10.	Judaism has civilized mankind.	TF	KBSF
11.	Anti-semitism is the non-Jew's hatred of God's message and His messengers.	TF	KBSF
12.	By and large, Israel has treated the Palestinians unfairly.	TF	KBSF
13.	The world media treats Israel objectively.	TF	KBSF
14.	Israel should take great risks for peace.	TF	KBSF
15.	Scientists are objective.	TF	KBSF
16.	Scientists are not defensive about accepting that there is a God.	TF	KBSF
17.	Many of my ideas and opinions come from my society.	TF	KBSF
18.	The women's role in Judaism is not sexist.	TF	KBSF
19.	Bible critics have found problems that can discredit the divinity of Torah.	TF	KBSF
20.	God is perfect. There is nothing He needs from human beings.	TF	KBSF
21.	God created me for pleasure.	TF	KBSF
22.	It is an honor and privilege to be able to keep the mitzvos.	TF	KBSF
23.	Whoever takes the Torah seriously will become great.	TF	KBSF
24.	The pleasure of one mitzvah is greater than all the pleasures available in this world.	TF	KBSF
25.	If you don't know what you would be willing to die for, you don't know what to live for.	TF	KBSF
26.	Evolution is a more reasonable explanation for the origin of the universe than the Biblical account.	TF	KBSF

27.	God could have created the world to appear millions of years old, from its inception.	TF	KBSF
28.	Chazal were objective.	TF	KBSF
29.	Assimilation cannot be reversed.	TF	KBSF
30.	God does not care if the majority of His children disappear.	TF	KBSF
31.	God loves frum Jews more than non-observant Jews.	TF	KBSF
32.	If God will help us, any problem can be solved.	TF	KBSF
33.	We need to have goals in learning to get the most out of our learning time.	TF	KBSF
34.	The Yetzer Hora is always trying to get me to make a counterproductive choice.	TF	KBSF

COMMON MISCONCEPTIONS
THAT ALIENATE PEOPLE
FROM TORAH

While the nonobservant person may intellectually perceive Judaism as beneficial for his life, various emotional blocks could be holding him back from getting involved.

In order to help people grow, it is critical to expose the fallacies that cause them to limit their involvement with Judaism. We have identified four common areas of difficulty and approaches to overcoming them.

A. The Perception: *If I were to become "religious," I would have to give up some of life's most cherished pleasures. Religion restricts your enjoyment of life. Why would I choose to do that (especially if I'm already happy with my life. . . .)?*

Step 1: *Correct the Mistake*

You must reassure the nonobservant person that becoming frum does not mean giving up pleasure. Quite the contrary. In Judaism, we are encouraged to marry, have children, eat, drink and take pleasure in the world around us. Jewish tradition places great emphasis on "simcha" — joy — and on the abundant opportunities for celebration. Our holiday gatherings are replete with good food, song, dance and exuberant rejoicing.

God created the entire world for our pleasure. Just as parents want only the best for their children, so does our Father in Heaven want only the best for us.

That is why He gave us the Torah.

Imagine someone gave you a state-of-the-art food processor, with a whole variety of gadgets and features that let you prepare exquisite dishes with ease and efficiency. If you ignore the instruction manual and never learn how to use all the features, or worse, if you use the machine as a paperweight, your enjoyment of it will be extremely limited. You will spend most of your time doing tasks that could be done for you by the machine and instead use only a fraction of its potential.

God wants us to go through life first class. So He gave us an instruction manual (the Torah) to show us how to get the most out of life; how to use everything in the world to get the maximum pleasure.

Becoming observant doesn't mean giving up pleasure. Just the opposite. *Without Torah, one cannot experience all of life's pleasures.* In giving up illusions for real pleasure, the opportunities to "have it all" are expanded beyond computation. All one has to "give up" is the notion that physical pleasure is the only real pleasure people desire.

[Incidentally, Chazal tell us that for everything the Torah proscribes, God created a "kosher" equivalent.[1] There is, indeed, no pleasure in life that cannot be obtained through Judaism.]

---

1. Chulin 109b

Step 2: *Explain How the Misconception Arose*

Many people unknowingly attribute certain "Christian" concepts to Judaism, since their impressions of Judaism are filtered through the broader medium of religion in society, which is predominantly Christianity. In reality, Judaism and Christianity are worlds apart. Celibacy and asceticism are Christian concepts. Judaism categorically rejects the view that abstinence from physical pleasures is necessary to acquire spirituality.

B. THE PERCEPTION: *Orthodox Jews look down on us. They don't respect us as Jews. We're not good people in their eyes simply because we don't keep the rituals as they do.*

Step 1: *Correct the Mistake*

Judaism teaches that only God can judge people. All we can judge are specific actions: it is wrong to murder, it is wrong to steal. But we have no way of knowing which Jew is better than another or which Jew is more beloved by God.

There's an old saying, "It's not where you are on the ladder, it's how many rungs you have climbed." It is possible that one deed performed by a secular Jew could have more merit in God's eyes than 100 mitzvos done by an observant person.

Torah law itself shows us this.

One Jew cannot kill another Jew to save his own life — even if that other Jew is a thief, a drug addict or a murderer.

The principle behind this, says the Talmud, is that we do not know "whose blood is redder."[2] We cannot judge the value of another Jew.

If you want to be successful in kiruv, you must reassure people, through your words, your attitude and your tone of voice, that you do not look down on them and that you are not judging them. When someone tells you, "I am a good Jew at heart," he is often in need of reassurance that you respect him despite any disagreements you have about his lifestyle.

Step 2: *Explain How the Misconception Arose*

This attitude of condescension is not unique to Orthodox Jews. It exists across the entire religious spectrum and derives from the human need to be "right." It is a common defensive reaction to look down on another human being whose beliefs are not your own. It may exist where people do not feel confident that they have a belief which will stand up to scrutiny. This syndrome can be found in secular, Orthodox, or Reform Jews. Those who believe they have a religious license to devalue other people for any reason have a skewed understanding of Judaism. Plain and simple.

At the same time, however, being an openminded person does not mean that one accepts each and every opinion without investigation and analysis. It simply indicates a willingness to listen to any argument based on logic and evidence. One cannot condemn Orthodox Jews for holding their convictions firmly, provided a) those beliefs are based on investigation and reason,

---

2. Pesachim 25b

and b) that they do not derogate those who do not share those beliefs.

Only God knows the potential and trials of each individual, and only He can judge the level of righteousness of a human being. Only God knows exactly how many rungs of the ladder each of us has ascended.

C. The Perception: *If I find out Torah is true, I'll have to keep it all. I'll never be able to do that, so why get started in the first place?*

Step 1: *Correct the Mistake*

This attitude implies that unless one keeps the entire Torah, it is not worthwhile doing just one mitzvah.

This is a fallacy.

One mitzvah has infinite value. Even if all you can do is one mitzvah, you will gain something eternal, something more worthwhile than anything in this world.

If you stumbled across a gold mine, would you refuse to take the gold simply because you know you won't find *all* the gold mines in the world? That one mine alone will make you a rich man for life!

A mitzvah is a gold mine. It will enrich your life immeasureably. Even if you do just one.

What invariably happens, though, is that after the non-observant person does one mitzvah, he finds it easier to take on another and another. Once the door to a relationship with God is opened, the strength to continue often comes naturally.

Step 2: *Explain How the Misconception Arose*

The "all or nothing" view is not Jewish. It typifies Christian theology, in which "believing in Jesus" is the sole criterion for admission to Heaven. Without that, a lifetime of good deeds does not make an individual worthy of reward.

In Judaism, every mitzvah is intrinsically meaningful, and every good deed will be rewarded, regardless of what percentage of the entire Torah is upheld.

The notion of "If I can't keep the whole Torah, I'm a failure," is also mistaken. Many people have internalized the Western definition of success, which takes the "all or nothing" approach: If I don't succeed, I have, de facto, failed. Effort and growth are irrelevant.

Judaism begins with the premise that "Ain tzaddik ba'aretz asher yaaseh tov v'lo yechetah." There is no one who will be able to accomplish it all; every human being is fallible.

Success in Jewish terms, therefore, means growth and effort. A person who makes a sincere attempt is a spiritual success, regardless of what he accomplishes quantitatively — and he should take pleasure in that success. On the other hand, a person who has a brilliant mind but does not exert himself to learn may not be a success in spiritual terms, even though he easily absorbs thousands of pages of Talmud.

Do not worry that you are watering down Judaism by advocating that a non-observant Jew take on one mitzvah at a time. Declaring that certain mitzvos *are no longer binding or obligatory* would be watering down Judaism. What we are doing here, however, is simply employing a technique to help the person begin to do mitzvos. We are in no way suggesting that the other mitzvos are not obligatory. Instead, we are encouraging the person to fulfill at least some of his obligations even if he can't fulfill them all.

D. The Perception: *I don't want to start learning, because if I learn and I don't observe, I'm worse off than if I had remained uneducated.*

Step 1: *Correct the Mistake*

When a person begins to learn, he is taking the first step in acknowledging a relationship with God, his Father in Heaven. Making this first "connection" is, in and of itself, unconditionally valuable. Even if fears or hesitations prevent him from doing any of the mitzvos, he is infinitely greater than if he does not acknowledge his Creator at all.

Second, the most important study anyone can engage in is the study of life itself. A person who understands more about life is certainly better off than one who knows little. "Toras Chaim," as we refer to our Torah, means "instructions for life." By deepening our understanding of Torah, our daily lives are enriched and our vision of life is expanded — even if we never actually become observant.

Step 2: *Explain How the Misconception Arose*

If we compare our relationship with God, our Father in Heaven, to our relationship with our parents, the fallacy in this rationalization becomes apparent.

If your father gave you an assignment that you did not feel like doing, which response do you think he would prefer?

"Dad, I want to listen to you but I am just not up to doing it right now,"

or,

"You're not my father! You have no right to ask anything of me! I don't want any relationship or involvement with you. Goodbye."

Any parent would rather be in touch with his child, even if that child is disobedient, because the alternative — being cut off from the relationship — is far worse than any amount of disobedience. As long as the channels of communication are open, the possibility of developing and improving the relationship remains open.

Chazal tell us that Torah learning is greater than all other mitzvos, because learning leads to action and action leads to change. Learning about God and initiating even a minimal relationship with Him, is of critical importance for every Jew, even if he refuses to commit himself to keeping Torah in a tangible way. Having a relationship with God is the Jew's first step toward immortality. There can be no greater loss than closing the door on this priceless opportunity.

Note: Although for an observant Jew, it is sometimes better to remain in the category of "shogeg," (inadvertent) rather than "mayzid" (knowing) with respect to committing avairos, this formula would not apply to the secular Jew. Since the latter has no attachment to God at all, it is better for him to learn about Torah and mitzvos, even if he chooses not to uphold them, rather than to remain totally cut off from his Creator.

How to Answer Questions

In doing outreach you are likely to encounter two types of questioners.

The first type is sincerely interested in acquiring information about Judaism.

The second, although he may phrase his statements in the form of a question, is not truly seeking an answer. His goal is to attack your position and "stump" you, in order to justify his opposition to your beliefs.

The first person can be dealt with in a straightforward way. He is interested in listening to what you have to say.

The second questioner requires a different type of response. Answering him in a standard way will not be helpful because he is not ready to evaluate your position objectively. You must first catch his attention by pointing out flaws in his reasoning which demonstrate that he does not fully understand the issue.

To do this, you need to expose an *internal contradiction within his own viewpoint*. It will not be effective simply to give evidence substantiating your view. More than likely, he has already heard the rationale behind your position and has formulated answers and rationalizations to dismiss it.

The Torah (in Parshas Vayigash) gives us a stunning example of this technique in action.

When Joseph's brothers sold him into slavery, they committed two avairos, one directly and one indirectly.

The direct avaira was selling Joseph. In doing this, they also indirectly became guilty of the avaira of causing anguish to their father Jacob.

Many years later, when the brothers went to Egypt to buy food, Joseph "framed" them for theft and forced them to bring Benjamin down in order to vindicate themselves. Joseph wanted to place his brothers in a situation which would test their loyalty to Benjamin and to their father, in order to determine if they had honestly regretted their earlier sins of having sold him.

When he could no longer withhold his identity, Joseph revealed himself with the following words,

"Ani Yosef. Ha'od avi chai?"

"I am Joseph. Is my father still alive?"

The phrase, "Is my father still alive?" was intended as one final reproach to the brothers, to draw their attention to the avaira against their father Jacob, which they incurred by selling Joseph.

The obvious question is, why did Joseph's rebuke focus on the seemingly "lesser" avaira of causing pain to Jacob? Shouldn't the logical, reflex-response have been,

"I am Joseph. *Why did you sell me into slavery?*"

Why invoke the avaira against Jacob right here and now?

One explanation is that Joseph understood that the most obvious angle would be the least effective in breaking down his brothers' defenses and getting them to admit their mistake. By this time, the brothers would have rationalized their actions and have come up with excuses to justify it. If Joseph would have said, "Why did you do this to me?" they would likely have responded with, "You deserved it," or, "You were a liar," or, "You were liable for the death penalty," etc. The brothers had plenty of time to prepare their answers to this question, and Joseph would not have succeeded in showing them their error.

In asking "Is my father still alive?" Joseph challenged them on a completely different level, one for which they had not built up defenses. Joseph reproached them for the avaira of causing anguish to Jacob, and the brothers had no response. In focusing their attention on a clear and indefensible mistake, Joseph got his brothers to recognize that their reasoning in the entire affair was flawed. Thus, he enabled them to view the entire incident in an objective, honest light.

The same principle applies to the questioner who aims to attack your position. First point out the flaws in *his* reasoning. This will show him that his own contention is not well founded. Then you will have opened him up to consider new information on the issue. If he is intellectually honest, he will be interested in determining the truth. You will then be able to present your ideas to a person who is ready to consider them.

Regardless of which type of questioner you are facing, you must always remain patient and calm. Allow the person as much time as he needs to ask his question or express his opinion. Never cut him short. Nothing will make him reject your answer faster than the fact that you did not give him the courtesy of a full hearing before responding.

To illustrate the technique outlined above, we cite some common "attacks" on Torah Judaism, and some direct rebuttals that have proven to be effective. Please keep in mind that these are not complete answers to the contentions; they are only responses which are likely to make the person withdraw from his attacking mode and begin to consider the issue from a fresh perspective.

1. Comment: *I don't believe in absolute truth.*

   Response: Are you *absolutely* sure? If you say that those who believe in absolute truth are wrong and that only your point of view is correct, you're making an *absolute* statement about reality!

   Furthermore, if I say there is a G-d and you say there isn't, does G-d suddenly come into being for me and disappear for you? Obviously there can only be one reality.

2. Comment: *The Holocaust was a hoax made up by the Jewish establishment in order to evoke pity for them from the world community.*

   Response: What was the claim of the defendents who were tried and convicted at the Nuremberg Trials? Not that the Holocaust did not happen, but that they were not responsible since *they were only following orders.* Although their very lives were at stake, even *they* didn't say that it did not happen, and it certainly wasn't because lying was beneath them! It was simply not possible to do so.

3. Comment: *I'm turned off to Orthodox Judaism because I know an Orthodox Jew who cheated me in business.*

   Response: Which synagogue do you attend? I think you should resign your membership there because I know a Reform Jew who cheated in business.

   Obviously one thing has nothing to do with the

other. One Jew's moral lapse is not a reflection of Torah's validity. The fact that a Jew stole, for example, does not mean that the Torah is flawed. It simply means he was not following the Torah at that time.

4. Comment: *I don't accept Orthodox Judaism, because I believe in pluralism.*

   Response: Does that mean you would accept Jews for Jesus as a legitimate branch of Judaism? If not, then you are similar to Orthodox Jews, who also place limits on their pluralism. We need to clarify, what, by definition, renders a belief into a schism instead of a legitimate expression of Judaism.

Evidence for God's Existence and Torah Mi'Sinai

INTRODUCTION
TO TEACHING EVIDENCE
FOR GOD'S EXISTENCE
AND TORAH MI'SINAI

Imagine you've taken your car to a mechanic for a tuneup. The mechanic tells you that he can "feel the needs" of your car by placing his hands on its hood while the engine is running. Based upon this method of diagnosis, he concludes that you need a new carburator, and recommends one that will cost you $300 (not including labor).

Obviously, you would dismiss his recommendation out of hand because it is not based on any solid facts.

Now if we would refuse to rely on someone else's "intuition" when the risk is only $300, it is quite reasonable to expect that people will require more than feelings or premonitions when they consider life's most important questions such as "Is there a God?" and "What does He want from me?" In order to influence someone to change their beliefs, it will be necessary, therefore, to provide clear, convincing evidence as to why the Torah alternative is not only superior but true.

To fully appreciate this, it is important to understand the mindset of the secular Jew. To him, religion is the antithesis of science and reason; science is based upon fact, while religion is based upon blind faith and superstition.

This perception evolved as a result of Christianity's historical hostility to science. One of the most famous displays of this closemindedness occurred when Galileo discovered that the earth revolved around the sun, and not the other way around. Galileo's finding was censored by the Vatican because it conflicted with Christian doctrine.[1]

Unfortunately, Judaism has historically been lumped together with Christianity in the popular mind, as being anti-science and anti-reason. Therefore, it becomes counterproductive to suppress a desire for evidence, since this serves to reinforce the mistaken notion that Judaism, too, is anti-intellect and anti-science.

Furthermore, relying on "the faithfulness and credibility of our mesorah" as a method of fostering commitment is not effective.[2] Since most secular Jews have not considered what mesorah means and how it truly is a substantive way of justifying our belief system, they can not appreciate its value. To them it seems like just another form of "blind faith," or "tradition," a la *Fiddler on the Roof.*

We have found that people are sometimes reluctant to teach evidence for God's existence because they feel that providing intellectual evidence reduces the reality of God's existence to a logical theorem and trivializes Judaism.

---

1. Encyclopedia of Philosophy, Vol. 3, Pg. 263, MacMillan, NY 1972

2. See Igros Moshe, Yoreh Deah, Siman 71, which discusses the importance of clearly understanding the foundations of our faith and of teaching that information to students, rather than relying solely on the concept of mesorah.

This is indeed true for an observant Jew, who not only believes in Hashem, but has experienced His presence, whether through davening or Shabbos or learning Torah. For this Jew, limiting an awareness of Hashem to "scientific reasoning" deprives him of a much greater, more meaningful religious experience.

However, a Jew who does not believe in God must first be convinced of His existence before he can begin to work on developing a relationship with Him. In his case, intellectual evidence is a necessary foundation for an appreciation of Judaism and a relationship with God, rather than a trivialization.

Everyone understands that it would be absurd to limit one's appreciation of his mother to an analysis of genetic similarities. Someone who has been raised and cared for in his mother's home should have progressed much further. But an *adopted* child, who is trying to determine the identity of his natural mother, cannot be expected to create this relationship without real evidence that a particular woman is his mother.

Finally, while there may be a slight risk in teaching evidence to religious people because an occasional person may get confused, there is no such risk in offering "evidence" to nonbelievers. Since they do not believe in God to begin with, logical evidence can only enhance their commitment.

A final note: In determining the authorship of the Torah, there are only two possible options: Either God wrote it or man did.

Our aim in presenting evidence is not to convince the student beyond any doubt that God *must* have written the Torah. Our goal is to demonstrate that it is overwhelmingly more reasonable and credible that God wrote the Torah than that man did.

Second, it is easier for a person to evaluate the merits of a position when that position is contrasted with alternative scenarios. Analyzing all the possibilities for authorship of the Torah, therefore, makes it easier for a person to decide which possibility makes the most sense. When teaching this material, constantly remind your student of this. Ask him: Based on the available evidence, which position makes more sense? Could a human being have written this, or was it God?

INTRODUCTION TO HISTORICAL ARGUMENT

The foundation of Judaism is a *mesorah* — a national-historical tradition based on the fact that every Jew alive at the time of Matan Torah (the giving of the Torah) personally experienced God speaking to the assembled Jewish nation. It was not the miracles that accompanied this revelation, but the *unbroken, 3,300 year transmission of this experience*, which stands as the single greatest demonstration of the truth of Judaism's claim that God gave the Torah to the Jews and through them, to the entire world.

Eyewitnesses and Historical Events

How do we know that any national history is an account of events which actually happened?

In general, our ability to verify historical accounts is based on the use of various kinds of evidence, the most important of which is the number of eyewitnesses that are said to have been present at the event. Large numbers of claimed eyewitnesses is the most essential prerequisite for verifying the truth of any historical occurrence.

Based upon this critical standard — the number of claimed eyewitnesses — we can proceed to divide historical claims into four broad categories:

Types of Historical Claims

Type A: Personal Experience of One Person

We will define a Type A claim as one which claims to describe the personal experience of a single individual. Thus, if the claimed event actually occurred, this individual would have been the only eyewitness, and this event's claim to historical validity would rest solely on his testimony.

Type B: Small Groups Experiencing an Event

A Type B claim will be defined as one which purports to describe the experience of a small group of participants or eyewitnesses, numbering anywhere between two and a thousand.

Type C: Events Experienced by Large Numbers

A Type C claim is one which maintains that a very large number, roughly 50,000 or more, participated in or witnessed a certain event. Only a Type C claim, of the three mentioned so far, has even the possibility of being a national historical claim. Obviously, the greater the number of people involved, the more veracity can be applied to the claim.

Type D: Events Experienced by an Entire Nation

Which Claim Makes the Most Sense?

From the point of view of a person or group trying to

get others to accept a claim, each of these has certain advantages and disadvantages:

Type A

Type A claims, by their very nature, are completely outside the realm of verifiability. Anyone maintaining such a claim is inherently suspect precisely because there is no way that it can be independently verified. The advantage to a claimant trying to pull off a Type A hoax, obviously, is that there is no way of disproving the claim. Therefore, there is no great difficulty in making such a claim, even if nothing at all had actually occurred. Nor would there be any problem in greatly exaggerating a minor event which really did occur into a much more impressive story.

Type B

A Type B claim has the disadvantage of being suspect because there are so few eyewitnesses, but it does have an advantage over a Type A claim, since it has at least some chance of being verified, depending on the credibility of the particular eyewitnesses. The difficulty factor in getting people to believe a Type B claim which is an outright lie, or a convincing exaggeration, would seem to fall somewhere between a Type A claim and a Type C claim.

Type C

A Type C claim is completely within the realm of historical verifiability. It has a tremendous advantage — if the event the claim is based on actually occurred —

because the truth can be testified to by tremendous numbers of eyewitnesses. Moreover, when an event is part of an entire nation's history, it will soon become an unquestioned national historical fact since so many individuals in the national group will be testifying to the event's occurrence as well as telling their children about it.

These kinds of historical facts constitute most of what is commonly known as world history. Examples of such historical facts include: George Washington's tenure as the first President of the United States of America, Julius Caesar's life history, the Battle of Marathon, the rise and fall of the Roman Empire, and the French Revolution.

If, however, a person were to attempt to make a Type C claim for an event that never actually occurred or seek to magnify an insignificant event, he would be faced with the tremendously difficult task of getting hundreds of thousands of people to believe that they were eyewitnesses to events that never actually happened.

Type D

A Type D historical claim is clearly the easiest kind to verify. If it is true, then everyone in the national group will know it at the deepest level of knowledge, since everybody in the group was actually there. There will obviously be no need to present any additional evidence to anyone of that generation. The next generation will know that the event occurred, both because their own parents who were direct eyewitnesses told them, and because everyone else in the nation is either a direct eyewitness or the offspring of a direct eyewitness.

It is hard to imagine that this event would ever pass from the nation's memory, even hundreds or thousands of years later, because of the profound impact this event would have on the nation's consciousness.

As strong as the advantages of a Type D claim are, the disadvantages are absolutely devastating if the event never happened at all, if only a much less impressive event actually did take place, or if the number of eyewitnesses was substantially less than claimed. How would it be possible to fool an entire nation into believing that they themselves experienced something which either never happened or which had been completely misrepresented to them? How could they have been so totally fooled that they would all relate the falsehood to their children as if it were their own personal experience? Even if a very large section of the nation were able to be duped and even if a large portion were convinced to the extent that they actually passed on the lie to their children as if it was their own personal experience — even this would not yield a believable, communicable, verifiable national truth, because the next generation would find many amongst them who either denied the universal character of the national claim or were never told about it by *their* parents.

Perhaps we can better appreciate the tremendous disparity between these different types of claims by imagining the following scene.

A man is walking along the beachfront, followed by a single line of 100 blindfolded men, each with one hand on the shoulder of the man in front of him. Should we view this group as a collection of independent thinkers, each deciding for himself which direction to walk in, or is it really one leader followed by one hundred followers?

Imagine ten men each walking independently. Do they not represent a stronger statement about which way to go than the one hundred men being led by one leader?

If the chain of blindfolded men behind the one leader grew to one thousand or even one million, it would still be no more impressive an occurrence since each is not independently choosing which way to go, instead relying on the man in front of him in line, who in turn is relying on the man in front of him.

What emerges from all of this is that in evaluating the relative strengths of various types of historical claims, the key number to keep in mind is not the number of people who at some later date came to accept this claim as true, but the number of people it is claimed were direct participants or eyewitnesses.

Other Religious Claims

All of the world's major religions, with the exception of Judaism, display a surprisingly consistent pattern: Each predicates its beliefs entirely upon historical claims which are completely unverifiable. All of the world's major religions, with the sole exception of Judaism, are based on "Type A" claims.

Other Kinds of Historical Evidence

Besides the essential prerequisite of numbers of

claimed eyewitnesses or participants, there are other important factors necessary for reliable historical verification. In order for the truth and reliability of any event to be recognized by later generations, it is necessary for an historical tradition to have been preserved and passed down through written records or oral traditions *which have been fully accepted as true by the nation itself.* In addition, independent corroboration and archeological evidence both lend strength to historical claims, although neither are critical prerequisites for reliable verification.

Given the fact that every single one of the world's religions, aside from Judaism, lacks the crucial prerequisite of large numbers of eyewitnesses to the claimed events upon which the religion is based, they are completely outside the realm of historical or logical verification. Therefore, "faith" aside, it is not possible to prove or to know any of these other religions to be true.

Judaism, however, is entirely different. Acceptance of its reality does not necessitate faith. The Revelation to the Jewish people at Mt. Sinai is an event which was experienced not only by great numbers, but by the entire nation. In short, it is at least as verifiable as any other major event in world history.

The Role of Miracles

It is important to note that it is specifically Judaism, among all of the world's major religions, which attributes no significance whatsoever to claims of miracles as a basis for establishing a religion. Thus, for the Jew, the fact that Christianity claims Jesus performed miracles in front of small groups of people has absolutely no bearing on the validity of the religion at all.

The Rambam, (Rabbi Moshe Ben Maimon, also known as "Maimonides") states this emphatically in his codification of Jewish Law, the *Mishna Torah*:

> . . . Israel did not believe in Moses, our teacher, because of the miracles he did. For when one's emunah (belief or realization) is based on miracles, a lurking doubt always remains in the "heart" (mind or understanding) that it is possible that these signs were performed with the aid of special occult powers and/or witchcraft. All of the miracles that were performed by Moshe in the desert, he did because they were necessary, and not as a proof of his prophecy . . . What then was the basis of their (the Jewish people's) emunah? The Revelation at Mt. Sinai, which we saw with our own eyes, and heard with our own ears, not having to depend on the testimony of others . . . and therefore it says, 'Face to face, God spoke with you (the Jewish people).'

The Rambam here sets forth the fundamental principle of the historical argument.

> The revelation at Sinai itself is the sole proof that Moses' prophecy (the entire Torah) is truth . . . Before this event they didn't "believe" with an emunah which would have endured forever, but only with a belief that would have eventually been followed by doubts and speculation . . .

It should be noted here that the "doubts and specu-

lation" which Maimonides was so certain would have
eventually appeared amongst the Jewish people had
the Revelation at Sinai not taken place, would have
been expected *despite all the other miracles which
the entire nation had experienced,* including the Ten
Plagues, the splitting of the Red Sea, and the 40 years
of miraculous sustenance in the Sinai Desert.

Given the Rambam's view of the inadequacy of a
claim which would have been based even on the full
national experience of all the other miracles, with the
single exception of Matan Torah, it is easy to understand Judaism's disdain of the claims which other
religions make (i.e. Type A or B claims).

Does it make sense that God would expect us to
make the most important decision in our lives — i.e.,
what is His purpose or plan for us? — without the necessary evidence for us to make a logical, well thought
out decision?

Moreover, why would God establish His entire relationship with a nation through one man, without any
possibility of verification, and still expect this nation
to obediently follow an entire system of instructions,
based only on blind faith?

Finally, if God had actually communicated to man
in this way, how could we be expected to discover the
one true path amidst the confusion of all the various
competing religious world-views and claims of truth?
All of them would be Type A claims and therefore
completely impossible to verify.

It is obvious that God would not expect or even
want any people to follow a path to Him based on what
might be nothing more than dazzling magic tricks.

Establishment of Moses' Reliability as a Prophet

The Revelation at Sinai is vividly described in the Torah (Exodus 19:16 — 20:19):

> . . . and it came to pass on the third day (of the Jewish people's encampment at Mt. Sinai) in the morning, that there were thunderings and lightenings and a thick cloud upon the mountain, and the sound of a shofar exceedingly loud; so that all the people in the camp trembled. And Moses brought the people out of the camp to meet with God; and they stood at the foot of the mountain. And Mt. Sinai smoked in every part, because the L-rd descended upon it in fire; and the smoke of it ascended like the smoke of a furnace, and the whole mountain quaked greatly. . . .

God then called to Moses to warn the people against coming too close to the mountain during the Revelation itself.

> . . . So Moses went down to the people, and spoke to them.

And immediately afterwards, while Moses was with the people at the bottom of the mountain . . .

> And God spoke all these words, saying . . .

The Torah goes on to list the Ten Commandments which together embody all of the basic principles of Judaism.

The fact that the first two of the commandments are written in the second person (i.e. God speaking directly to the Jewish people) rather than the third-person form of the final eight, is consistent with our Oral Tradition. Our Oral Tradition states that the Jewish people were only able to bear the intensity of God's presence long enough to receive the first two of the Ten Commandments directly from God Himself:

> . . . And all the people perceived the thunderings, and the lightenings, and the sound of the shofar, and the mountain smoking; and when the people saw it, they were shaken and stood afar off. And they said to Moses, you speak with us and we will hear: but don't let God speak with us, lest we die. And Moses said to the people, Fear not: for God has come to test you, in that His fear (realization) may be before your faces, that you err not. And the people stood afar off, and Moses drew near to the thick darkness where God was. . . .

This event — the verification of Moses' reliability as a prophet, through God's direct communication to the Jewish nation — is the foundation of the entire Jewish mesorah. Why else would God, Who has endowed human beings with a tremendous capacity for rational decision-making, expect, on demand, that an entire people follow a prophet, unless He had given them clear evidence of that prophet's reliability?

Therefore, the first command God gives to Moses after the Revelation is to transmit a critically important message to the Jewish people, directing them never to forget, regardless of their situation, what they had just experienced as a nation:

> . . . Thus you shall say to the Children of Israel —

You (plural) have seen that I have talked with you (plural) from heaven. . . .

This unique aspect of the Revelation — that it was *you* (each individual of the entire Jewish people) that saw, *you* that heard, *you* that personally experienced the Revelation — this aspect is absolutely fundamental to all of Judaism.

In fact, in Moses' final, 37-day speech to the entire Jewish people, delivered just before he died[1], Moses repeats and emphasizes this point no less than ten times.

Only Judaism Claims a National Revelation

This idea, that the basis of our knowledge of the truth of the Torah is the national Revelation at Mt. Sinai (a Type D event), is critical: it is what sets Judaism's claim apart from the claims of every other religion. It is what makes Judaism's claim a logical one (since it makes sense for God to have revealed His instructions in this manner), and it is what gives only Judaism even the possibility of historical verifiability. This has been the strength of the Jewish people, and the basis of their ability to follow the Torah way of life for the past 3,300 years. No other religion can be evaluated based on evidence; you either take the prophet's word on faith, or you don't.

Since it makes sense that other religions would also seek to base their claims on "solid" ground, we would expect them all to make claims similar to the

---

1. Related in the Book of Deuteronomy

Jewish one (or at the very least Type B or C claims) —
in other words, claims with at least the possibility of
being logically verified.

How do we account for the fact that not a single one
does?

Moreover, instead of professing a Type C or Type D
claim, which would have been their best bet for serious
consideration, the world's many and varied religions
all amazingly abandoned any hope of credibility at all
by making the least logical and, by definition, unverifiable claim that God communicated His will to all of
mankind, through a Type A claim of only one man.

Virtually every major aspect of the Torah has been
borrowed or copied by the non-Jewish world: circumcision, mikvas (baptism), dietary restrictions, Shabbos,
the Sabbatical year (even university professors see
the wisdom of this Torah concept). Modern Western
social and legal systems are largely based on Torah
foundations. Social equality, criminal justice, charity,
brotherhood, labor laws, fair-wage guidelines, and loving one's neighbor are all derived from the Torah that
the Jewish people received from God 3,300 years ago.
Moreover, there is nothing more central to western
civilization than the belief in one God and the Ten
Commandments! In sum, we find that many major
ideas and concepts of the Torah have been lifted, either
directly or with some modification, by other religions,
*except for the one idea which is the very foundation of
the entire system!*

But this is not surprising to the Jewish people. The
fact that the sole concept in Torah which non-Jews
have never attempted to expropriate is the Jewish
claim of a national revelation was explicitly prophesied

by Moses in one of his final messages to the Jewish people shortly before his death 3,300 years ago.

In a direct challenge to future generations, to carefully examine all of world history to see that no other nation on earth has ever made a claim of National Revelation, Moses declares,

> For ask now of the days that are past, which were before you, since the day that God created man upon the earth, and from one side of heaven to the other, whether there has been any such thing as this great thing, or whether anything has been heard like it? Did ever people hear the voice of God speaking out of the midst of fire, as you have heard, and lived? Or has God ventured to go and take Him a nation from the midst of another nation, by trials, by signs, and by wonders, and by war, and by a mighty hand, and by a stretched out arm, and by great terrors, according to all that the Lord, your God did for you in Egypt before your eyes?

Moses was in fact the first to formulate the "historical" argument. If, as the Bible critics claim, the Torah is only a man made document, how could the authors promise that no other religion would ever make the claim of National Revelation? If the authors of the Torah could get away with it, why wouldn't anyone else?

> . . . To you it was shown that you might *know* that the Lord, He is God; there is none else besides Him. Out of heaven He caused you to hear His voice, that He might instruct you . . .

Moses is instructing us *all*, especially the generations in the "latter days":

"Understand this clearly, and never forget it: Two to three million of your ancestors stood at Mt. Sinai and heard God speak to them. The Jewish people have transmitted this truth to their children throughout the generations. No other religion has ever attempted to make a claim remotely approaching the Jewish one. These facts all stand as the basis of our knowledge that the Torah is from God."

Since God Himself designated Moses as His prophet before the entire Jewish people at Mt. Sinai, it logically follows that He can then give them mitzvos (instructions for living), through Moses. Since in all the other religions, no Divine endorsement of a leader was ever given to a group of people, no other religious leader can make a verifiable claim that God expects these groups to follow their leader's instructions.

This difference between Judaism and every other religion is the reason why the Torah can demand that the Jewish people attain *knowledge — intellectual clarity —* and not mere faith, in their relationship with God. It is precisely because our ancestors all stood at Mt. Sinai — precisely because a National Revelation claim can not be fabricated.

Knowledge and Emotion

> *Know* therefore this day, and consider it in your heart, that the Lord He is God in heaven above, and upon the earth beneath, there is no other . . .

Given the multitude of possible religions and "paths to God" clamoring for our attention and our human tendency to settle for half-truths and comfortable compromises to tough questions, we are instructed to rely primarily on our minds in our initial inquiry into reality.

However, as important as intellectual knowledge may be initially ["*Know* therefore this day"], it must be joined by emotional realization ["and consider it in your *heart*"].

This is the message conveyed in the verse cited above. For a complete relationship with God — one needs both intellect and emotion. Knowledge of God without feeling leaves a person disconnected, out of touch with his convictions. Feeling without knowledge, on the other hand, is the basis for every cult, nationalistic ideology, and charismatic movement in history. Both components together, intellect and emotion, are requirements for every Jew in his search for truth and a relationship with God.

How to Present
THE HISTORICAL ARGUMENT

Introduction:

The purpose of the following argument is to offer evidence for the Torah's claim that God spoke to the Jewish people on Mount Sinai, 3,300 years ago.

If you were to ask most Jews, "To whom did God speak on Mount Sinai?" the likely response would be, "Moses."

"And what were the Jewish people doing during that time?"

"Worshipping the Golden Calf."

Thanks to Cecil B. Demille's *The Ten Commandments*, most people take this mistaken rendering of the Torah's account as fact.

In reality, God gave the Torah to the entire Jewish nation on Mount Sinai. The Golden Calf incident took place later. (The movie never has all the facts; you have to read the Book!)

As the Torah states in Deuteronomy, Chapter 4, Verse 32:

> You might inquire about times long past, going back to the time that God created man on earth, [exploring] one end of the heavens to the other. See if anything as great as this has ever happened, or if the like has ever been heard. Has any nation ever

heard God speaking out of fire, as you have, and still survived? Has God ever done miracles bringing one nation out of another nation with such tremendous miracles, signs, wonders, war, a mighty hand and outstretched arm, and terrifying phenomena, as God did for you in Egypt before your very eyes?

You are the ones who have been shown; so that you will know that God is the Supreme Being, and there is none besides Him.

From the heavens, He let you hear His voice admonishing you, and on earth He showed you His great fire, so that you heard His words from the fire.

The Torah is making two distinct claims here.

First, that the entire Jewish people heard God speak to them at Mount Sinai.

Second, that no other nation, from the beginning of time till the end of time, would ever be able to make this claim.

Before we analyze the veracity of these claims, let us consider the following question.

If God were going to "introduce Himself" to a group of people and establish a religion for all time, which method would make more sense: To transmit it directly to each person individually, or to have Him appear to a prophet who, in turn, would transmit it to the people?

Obviously, if His concern was to instill unshakeable belief in His authority, He would give it to *all* the people.

Revealing Himself only to the prophet, would give the people no foolproof method of determining whether the revelation really happened or not. The people would have to take the prophet's word for it.

Now inasmuch as national revelation is the best claim with which to start a religion, why is it that

Judaism is unique amongst thousands of religions, in making this claim?

Furthermore, let us assume the Torah was written by a human author, who was forging the document, claiming to be God. Why predict that no other nation would make the claim of national revelation? He himself knows it's the best claim, and if he could fabricate it, why would he think others couldn't?

Oddly enough, to this very day, as we have seen previously, there has been no nation or religion other than the Jewish people that makes the claim of National Revelation as its founding experience.

There are two possible points in history when the Torah could have been given: Either at Mount Sinai, when the Torah claims it was given, or, at any other time in history.

Let's examine both of these possibilities.

A. *Mount Sinai.*

Assuming it was indeed given in the Sinai Desert 3,303 years ago, we'll say Moses and perhaps a committee of Bible authors went up to the mountain and spent forty days inventing and writing the Torah. Then they came down from the mountain with this Torah and presented it to the Israelites.

What do you think would have happened next?

Obviously, the Israelites would ask: "Moses, where'd you get it from?"

And Moses would answer, "Don't you remember? It says right here in this Torah, God gave it to *all of us* forty days ago."

Naturally, the people would reject this. They'd say, "What fools do you take us for? God didn't give us anything. How can you be so brazen?"

If they liked Moses, they would probably say, "Moses, we'd like to keep you as our leader. Why don't you go back up the mountain, erase this stuff about God giving Torah to *all* of us and instead say God revealed Himself to *you* and told *you* to present us with His Torah."

It is clear that nobody could make a fallacious claim of national revelation and ever hope to get away with it, because one can not lie regarding another person's personal experience.

In fact, this is so absurd, that even secular Bible critics don't hypothesize that Moses put forth a claim of national revelation to the generation in the desert.

This brings us to the next possibility.

B. *The Torah was given at a later date.*

Let's say Ezra the Scribe, or King Josiah appeared a thousand years after the author's date of revelation and presented the Jewish people with the Torah — a theory certain Bible critics subscribe to.

The people would ask, "Ezra, where'd you get this from?"

Ezra would say, "Read it. It says right here that God gave this Torah to the entire nation on Mount Sinai a thousand years ago."

Now the Jewish people would ask, "Where was this Torah yesterday? How come we've never seen it before? My father or grandfather never mentioned anything about it."

What would Ezra answer?

He would have to say that the event did indeed occur one thousand years ago, as the Torah says, but that it was forgotten.

First, how could such an earth-shattering event such as God revealing Himself to an entire nation be forgotten?

And second, not only is it impossible for a religion and nation to forget its founding experience, but the Torah itself promises that it will never be forgotten!

The Torah states in Deuteronomy, 31:21,

> When they are beset by many evils and troubles, this song shall testify for them like a witness, since it will not be forgotten by the mouths of their descendants.

If it had in fact been forgotten, that, in and of itself, would have disproved the claim of divine authorship. If God wrote the Torah, how could it be that His statement is proven false?

Therefore, at no time in our history would it have been possible for this fabrication to have been perpetrated. The fact that the majority of the Jewish people for the past three thousand years have accepted this claim as their history can only be because it is true.

And that is the reason why there is only one nation and one religion in the entire world that can make the claim of National Revelation.

THE PSYCHOLOGY OF CONTROL ARGUMENT

Introduction:

This argument demonstrates, through the use of simple human psychology, that it is highly unlikely for human beings to have written the Torah. In other words, if human authors were writing this Torah with the intention of passing it off as a divine document, there are certain laws and passages in it that would never have been included, because these laws would undermine the authors' own credibility and reveal that the true authors were not God, but people.

Let us imagine that we are living thirty three hundred years ago. We are members of a select committee to write the Torah, and I am your chairman. Our goal is to convince the people that this is a divine document given to us by God.

In addition to obvious laws, such as "Don't kill" and "Don't steal," I'd like to propose the following:

1. *Every seventh year the nation may not work the fields.* They may not gather produce or seed the ground. The gates to their fields must remain open to allow anyone to enter and take whatever they desire.

Can you think of any benefits such a law would offer?

An obvious one is that letting the fields lay fallow gives the soil an opportunity to replenish itself.

Another benefit is that this respite gives the people time to study the laws that we want them to follow.

But there's a problem: How are people going to study our laws if they are starving to death for lack of crops?

Can you think of any solutions to this problem so we can keep this law on the books and receive its benefits?

How about dividing the land into seven zones? Each year a different zone will rest.

What about importing food from neighboring countries?

No. I've got a better solution.

What if we just tell the people, "God promises that the sixth year will produce enough food for the sixth, seventh and eighth years."

What do you think of that idea?

Obviously we don't have control over how many crops the earth is going to produce. If we're pretending to be God, and we promise something we know we can't deliver, we will be exposed as frauds.

How long do you think this religion will last if we make this promise?

About six years.

Yet, this is exactly what the Torah commands!

The Torah states, in Leviticus 25:3-6:

For six years you may plant your fields, prune your vineyards, harvest your crops but the seventh year is the sabbath of the land in which you may not plant your fields nor prune your vineyards. Do not harvest crops that grow on their own. Do not gather the grapes on your unpruned vines since it is a year of rest for the land.

And if you ask, what will we eat in the seventh year? We haven't planted nor have we harvested crops. I will direct my blessing to you in the sixth year and the land will produce enough crops for three years.

Who could have written this? Who would make such a promise? Why would a group of authors who want people to believe in the divinity of this book make a promise they can not possibly fulfill and thereby destroy their own claim of divine authorship?

Perhaps you will suggest that the miracle be dependent on the merit of the Jewish people keeping the shmitta. This way, if the triple crop doesn't come about, we can always say they didn't deserve it.

But in that case, we should have promised them a triple crop in the *eighth* year, when we could have determined if they were deserving of it, not in the sixth year before the shmitta year comes!

2. My next idea is a law which will help us retain control over this nation. *Let's have them all come up to the Temple three times a year and offer sacrifices.* This will ensure that we are constantly reinforcing our religion and the authority of the priestly class.

Is this a good law?

What if I add that *all* males, even the soldiers defending our borders, must make this pilgrimage too — all at the same time?

Do you see any problems with this?

Obviously we are exposing ourselves to attack three times a year. Everyone, including our enemies, will discover exactly when our soldiers will be leaving to come to the Temple, and this law, instead of securing our sovereignty, will place it in jeopardy.

We can't rule a country once it's been conquered by another country!

How about exempting soldiers from this law?

Or having different districts come up to the Temple on different holidays? That would give us the benefits of the law and eliminate the dangers.

Yet, the Torah declares, (Exodus 34:23-24):

> Three times each year *all* your males shall thus present themselves before God the Master, the Lord of Israel. When I expel the nations before you and extend your boundaries, *no one will be envious of your land when you go to be seen in God's presence three times each year.*

The Torah's solution to the inherent dangers of this law is simply: "Don't worry. God will arrange that no one will be envious of your land."

Who could have written this law? How could any human being promise in writing something which requires powers totally beyond his control?

And furthermore, why would anyone be willing to risk his own credibility and the legitimacy of his religion, when in both these cases, it's so easy to come up with ways to keep the laws and eliminate the problems? Why couldn't the committee who was forging this document come up with similar solutions?

Finally, if they couldn't come up with solutions, why write these laws at all? They completely undermine the objective of creating the religion in the first place!

3. In its description of what makes an animal kosher,

the Torah states, (Leviticus 11:3): "Among the mammals you may eat: any one that has true hooves that are cloven and that chews its cud."

With this statement, we have all the information we need to determine if an animal is kosher or not: cloven hooves and chewing the cud.

However, the Torah elaborates.

> Of the cud-chewing animals and the hoofed animals, these are the only ones that you may not eat: The *camel* shall be unclean to you although it chews its cud, since it does not have a cloven hoof. The *shafan* shall be unclean to you although it chews its cud, since it does not have a cloven hoof. The *arnevet* shall be unclean to you although it chews its cud, since it does not have a cloven hoof. The *pig* shall be unclean to you although it has a cloven hoof, since it does not chew its cud. Do not eat the flesh of any of these animals. (Leviticus 11:4-8)

Question: If the Torah already gave us the specific signs to identify a kosher animal, why list these four exceptions? Obviously, these animals are not kosher. They don't fulfill the requirements. What is this new information adding to our understanding of the kosher laws?

Furthermore, the Torah explicitly tells us that these are the *only* four animals in the entire world that have one sign and not the other.

How would the authors have known that? Was Moses on American Sportsman on Saturday afternoons, hunting in the wilds of Africa?

By now, zoologists have identified over 5,000 different species of animals. Today there is no geographic area in the world that escapes man's careful scrutiny.

And yet, after all this time and throughout the entire universe, man has never found an animal that has one of the kosher signs and not the other, besides the four identified in the Torah. And, just as the Torah states, the only animal in the world that has true split hooves and does not chew its cud is the pig.

Now, if the authors of the Torah were human beings, with a limited understanding of the world and the animal kingdom, how is it possible that this claim has been corroborated thousands of years later in modern times? We know that at that time it was impossible to identify every existing mammal in the world. There were areas of the world that mankind had not yet even inhabited, and thousands of species whose existence at that time were unknown to man.

Furthermore, if human beings wrote the Torah, the one thing they knew for sure is that *they did not know all of the animals in existence.*

Why would they put the credibility of the Torah on the line by making such a statement?

If they had some strange reason for wanting us to keep kosher, they could have accomplished this without having to specify the precise number of animals in the world with only one sign and not the other.

No human being trying to pass off a forged Torah as divine would deliberately include statements which are bound to be proven false, and risk exposing himself as a fraud.

Who wrote this law?

Only a Supreme Being who can know for certain the characteristics of every animal in the world.

THE MORAL IMPERATIVE

**Why the Existence of Morality
Necessitates God's Existence**

Most people believe in the existence of a universal ethic
— that right and wrong are *real, objective* values which
prevail for all time and cut across every geographic and
societal boundary line; in short, that some things are
categorically good and others are unconditionally evil.

Where do these concepts of right and wrong come
from?

Anthropologists and sociologists have posited various theories as to the source of right and wrong. These
theories generally fall into three categories:

A) *Society.* Right and wrong are determined solely by
   the society in which we live. For example, incest is
   taboo because society has inculcated us to believe
   so.
B) *Survival.* Morality is essentially a social contract
   among members of society. The concept of "right"
   describes the means by which human society can
   survive and flourish. "Wrong" is that which is destructive to society.
   For example, since I do not want myself or my
   children to be killed, murder is wrong. Morality,
   then, is a convention arrived at in order to achieve a
   stable, cooperative society. For our mutual benefit

70

we have all agreed to live by certain rules; these rules classify actions as "right" and "wrong."

C) *Personal Taste.* Morality is simply an expression of personal taste or opinion. It is completely subjective. No external authority dictates it. For example, I like chocolate ice cream, you like vanilla. I like giving to charity, you don't.

We will now demonstrate that, upon closer examination, each of these explanations is flawed and therefore cannot be the catalyst of a universal morality ethic. Thus, if morality is real and absolute, the only remaining explanation for its existence must be that it is imbued within us by God, whose authority is timeless and absolute.

A) *Society.* While it is true that society does have a strong influence on the moral choices of its members, societies do not *create* their own moral principles. All societies, no matter how diverse, agree on many of the fundamental principles of morality. Individual societies merely *direct* the application of these principles.

To illustrate, consider the following:

At one time in Eskimo society, first-born daughters were routinely drowned because they were considered dependents, not breadwinners.

At first blush, this would appear to support the view that each society creates its own morality. After all, the Eskimos unabashedly commit acts that the Western world considers murder.

However, what would happen if an Eskimo were to drown his first-born *son?*

He would be considered a murderer by Eskimo society!

Why?

Because *taking an innocent life* is murder to the Eskimo. The first-born son is an innocent baby, not a parasite.

The taking of an innocent life is murder in any society. All that differs from one group to the next is the application of that principle — the interpretation of who is innocent.

What would Hitler call the man who would have killed Göring? No doubt, a murderer, even an assassin.

Why? Because to Hitler, Göring was an innocent man. The Jews were not "innocent," therefore killing them was not a violation of the moral principle proscribing murder.

The Eskimo, the Nazi and the common Western man all agree on the definition of murder: the taking of an innocent life. Although they could not disagree more in its application, all have a common understanding of this basic moral precept.

Extremely diverse societies, separated by thousands of miles, vastly different from each other in almost every cultural way, somehow share a common definition of murder.

How can this be?

If morality was a product of society, then diverse societies would create diverse moralities. But they don't. Even the most dissimilar communities have a uniform understanding of moral principles. The source for morality must therefore transcend society and culture.

B) *Survival.* One whose highest priority is survival will only make choices that he believes will somehow enhance or protect his prospects of staying alive. Yet the belief in right and wrong, in many, many instances, actually threatens physical survival. It can motivate an individual to sacrifice his wellbeing or even his life, in defense or fulfillment of a moral principle. How many great people throughout history have chosen to die rather than commit an evil act.

When asked, "Would you rather have been a guard or a prisoner in Auschwitz?" many people respond that they would rather have been the oppressed, than the oppressor.

When asked, "Which would you choose if you were forced to kill 100 innocent children or give up your own life?" most people say they believe (or at least hope) they would give up their own lives.

If right and wrong were products of the instinct to survive, then we would view as "good" only that which protects and preserves our lives. However, the desire to be moral seems to push us to do things which often put tremendous pressure and stress on our physical bodies, and in many cases leads us to risk or sacrifice our lives. How then, can the "survival" drive be the source of right and wrong?

C) *Personal Opinion.* One needs only to define the term "personal opinion" to realize that this could not plausibly be the force that has created a universal ethic.

A personal opinion is simply that: a reflection of one's individual likes and dislikes. No value judgment can be placed upon a personal opinion, and one's own preferences can never be absolute or binding upon another person.

For example, one who prefers vanilla ice cream over chocolate is not offended by a friend's choice of chocolate over vanilla; it is not *wrong* to prefer the chocolate, it is simply a matter of taste.

When it comes to matters of ethics, however, people do not maintain this attitude. When two parties disagree on an ethical issue, each believes the position of his friend is incorrect and objectively inferior to his own.

The only reasonable source, then, for a universal, eternal standard of right and wrong is a Being that fits that description. By definition, human beings are limited; their personal whims or opinions cannot create anything absolute or universally binding. Only God, who is outside of time and space, who is unaffected by the shifting sands of history and culture, can create a set of standards which, as an expression of His will, reflect universal and eternal truth.

Sometimes, when people begin to realize this, they switch gears and adopt the position that they do not believe in the existence of right and wrong at all. If there is no absolute morality, they cannot be led to the conclusion that God must enter the picture. In this case, you simply have to point out the overwhelming amount of evidence gleaned from the way they and others live, that clearly demonstrates their belief in right and wrong.

To clarify this point, imagine you are standing at the corner of a busy intersection. Cars are speeding by in all directions. A man stops you and tells you he actually thinks that you are both standing in the middle of a rain forest.

How do you determine if the man really believes what he is saying? Ask him to take a short stroll in the forest. If he refuses, or stalls until the light turns green, you know he really does see the cars. For his actions have belied his words and loudly articulated his true beliefs.

Similarly, when we deal with morality, people may say they do not believe in the existence of right and wrong, but their actions will invariably testify to the contrary. All people conduct their lives as though right and wrong are real values. If someone, God forbid, were to commit a terrible act of violence upon a loved one, no one would say, "Well, to each his own. The attacker has a right to do things his way. Some like chocolate ice cream, others like vanilla. . . ." Murder, rape and crimes against humanity are not treated as differences in personal taste.

Conclusion:

We all take right and wrong very seriously. We will, at times, make tremendous sacrifices for moral principles. We may spend large amounts of time and effort; some of us may even die for them. We never cease to evaluate the actions, morals and political positions of others. In conclusion, the manner in which we conduct our lives demonstrates that we are aware of an absolute standard of morality.

Judaism and Contemporary Issues

THE CHOSEN PEOPLE

The Jewish nation is often referred to in the Torah and prayerbook as "the Chosen People."

Many people find this term distressing. They believe the "Chosen People" concept is a racist idea. It seems suspiciously close to the Nazi concept of an "Aryan" nation. It appears to fly in the face of the Western ideal of all people being equal before God.

In truth, though, when the Torah refers to the Jews as having been "chosen," it is not in any way asserting that Jews are racially different or superior. Americans, Asians, Russians, Israelis, Europeans, Scandinavians and Ethiopians — caucasians, blacks and orientals — are all part of our nation. It is impossible to define the Jews as one monolithic race; Jews are as racially diverse as there are races!

But while the term "Chosen People" does not mean a racially superior people, it does imply a special uniqueness belonging to those who are part of the Jewish people.

What is this uniqueness?

When the Torah calls the Jewish people an "Am Nivchar[1]," (a "Chosen People") it describes a nation with a special closeness to God; a relationship which is qualitatively better than all the nations of the world.

Since it was the Jewish people who voluntarily accepted upon themselves the special mission of spreading knowledge of God to all the nations, they earned the privilege of a closer relationship with God.

---

1. Devarim 7:6

Was this privilege, then, unfairly bestowed? Not if the opportunity to accept the special mission and merit the concordant privileges was open to all the nations.

Privileges, in and of themselves, do not necessarily imply discrimination or favoritism. If a privilege is offered to everyone who is willing to pay the necessary price, no one can then claim that those who were willing to make that extra effort were granted the privilege unfairly.

For example: a child who refuses to wash up, brush his teeth and go to sleep can hardly claim that his siblings who did so are arrogant and racist for accepting the special prize offered by their parents to those children who followed the rules. Nor can the parents be called unjust or even preferential in their treatment. Each child was given the same opportunity. Their situations are the result of their choices. The results were in no way skewed in anyone's favor.

The Torah tells us that mankind was created to relate to God. However, after Adam's mistake in the Garden of Eden, the elevated level on which Adam related to God was no longer available naturally to Adam or to his descendants. If it was to be attained, it would have to be through the individual choices of each member of mankind.

The only person committed enough to attain this exalted level of relating to God was Abraham. As a result of Abraham's choices, God made a covenant with him and his descendants; a covenant that was not arbitrary but earned, through Abraham's efforts and dedication.

The Midrash relates that when the Jewish people were poised to become one nation at Mt. Sinai, God first offered the Torah to every nation of the world[2]. Of them all, only the Jewish people wanted His Torah and the privileged closeness that came as a result of their assuming the role of God's ambassadors to the world.

Although that was the final opportunity for entire nations as a group to become part of the Jewish people, the door was always left open for the individual. Any person, regardless of national or racial background, can merit the benefit of this privileged relationship with God by choosing to accept the Torah and become part of the Jewish nation.[3]

It is important to note, though, that while the Torah does consider the Jewish nation privileged because of its special mission, Judaism nevertheless has great respect and admiration for the righteous among the gentiles.

Chazal say (Tosefta, Sanhedrin 13), "The righteous of all nations have a share in the World to Come."

Tanna D'bei Eliyahu Rabbah 9 states: "I call heaven and earth as witnesses. Any individual, *whether gentile or Jew*, man or woman, servant or maid, can bring the Divine Presence upon himself in accordance with his deeds."

The Jewish people are universalists. Even though the Torah is unequivocal about the importance of accepting the key principles of Jewish faith, we are taught that a non Jew will be rewarded for any good act he does. In contrast, Christianity and Islam do not reward righteous or moral acts done by those who do not adhere to their beliefs.

---

2. Bamidbar Rabba 14:10
3. Derech Hashem, 2:4, 3:4

Even the calendar systems of Christianity and Islam reflect their exclusionary philosophies. Each begins with the birth of their respective religion; man's existence before that time is considered irrelevant.

The Jewish calendar, on the other hand, begins with the creation of Adam. For in Judaism, the world becomes meaningful with the creation of the first man. Humanity is worth accounting for, even though the Jewish religion was not yet born.

In summary, the Jewish concept of the chosen people is neither racist nor unfair. It is the result of making the hard choices and the willingness to accept additional responsibilities. Of the world's major religions, only Judaism can be considered universalistic. All those willing to make the effort and accept the responsibility can achieve the same special closeness to God and transmit that gift to their descendants.

All they have to do is to want it. Nothing else holds them back.

WOMEN IN JUDAISM

Introduction

Before we begin our analysis of the Torah laws concerning women, it is important to recognize that the manner in which one evaluates any Torah law will be greatly influenced by the view one has of the Torah's origin.

If one assumes that the Torah was written by man, then all the laws contained within it are the products of human minds. In that case, the laws have no absolute value. They are not inherently beneficial for all Jews in all situations. Instead, as products of a finite intelligence, they have limited applicability and depth. More specifically, if created by members of a male-dominated society, these laws could be interpreted as bearing a distinct bias against women.

If one believes the Torah to be divinely authored by God, however, then all of its laws are the products of the Divine Intelligence of an Infinite Being — for all time, in absolute justness and perfection. In that case, even if one does not understand the reasons for a particular law, one can know for certain that it is designed for the benefit of each and every individual throughout the generations.

If the kashruth laws, for example, are simply a man-made attempt at a healthful diet, then if it subsequently appears that a nonkosher food is more healthful, there would be no reason not to eat it. As the human innovation of a subjective mind, kosher food would have no overriding benefit or spiritual imperative.

However, if the Torah was written by God, who created all of mankind and gave the Jewish people a prescription for the best possible physical, emotional and spiritual well being, then the same kashruth laws take on a completely different meaning. Even if a nonkosher food seems to be more healthful, this does not change the absolute reality that kosher food is better for us — even if we do not perceive its benefits.

Once we have established that God wrote the Torah, we relate to His laws in a manner similar to the way a patient relates to his doctor. If a patient trusts in his doctor's expertise, he will take the prescribed medications regardless of whether or not he understands the physiological process by which it will cure him. He knows that the doctor recommends what is best for him.

Obviously, if the patient does not have confidence in his doctor, he will be suspicious of his recommendations. That is why before you choose a doctor, you look for evidence of his ability. You only develop trust after you have seen repeated displays of his competence. No one would expect you to have blind faith in your doctor.

The same is true with God and Torah. You are not expected to blindly accept that the Torah is a divine document. In order to make an informed decision, you need to consider all the available evidence for its authorship. However, if Torah is indeed true, nothing would be more tragic than having lived your life with only a limited understanding, while the perfect guide-book to greatness had been there all along for your benefit.

The Torah View of Women

People who believe that Torah is the work of human beings generally view the laws concerning women as a reflection of ancient man's appraisal of women as second-class citizens. They therefore feel compelled to seek out and expose every apparent inference of prejudice, inequality and subjugation of women, and use that as a valid license to reject Torah altogether.

However, if one understands that the Torah was written by an eternal, just God, who created both man and woman in His image, who gave each specific roles through which they could find maximum fulfillment, and who charged them equally with the responsibility of perfecting themselves and the world around them, then these laws take on a completely different meaning.

One then begins his analysis with the premise that the difference between the roles of men and women were divinely masterminded for the *benefit* of each, and that one's self-actualization can best be achieved through fulfillment of his or her unique role.

In analyzing the "women in Judaism" issue, we shall begin with a look at some of the narratives in the Torah concerning women, and try to establish the Torah's viewpoint of the potential, value and role of women in Judaism.

Women Can Reach Spiritual Levels
Equal to Men

One of the earliest accounts in Jewish history, which recounts the lives of Abraham and Sarah, demonstrates that women can achieve levels of prophecy surpassing that of the greatest men.

The Torah tells us that Sarah noticed that the behavior of Ishmael (the son of her maidservant, Hagar) was destructive. She therefore requested that he be sent away, so as not to spoil the spiritual atmosphere desired for the development of her own son, Isaac. Abraham was greatly distressed by her request and was filled with indecision, until God said to him, "All that Sarah says to you, listen to her voice." (Gen. 21:12)

Rashi explains that we learn from here that *Sarah was superior to Abraham in prophecy.*

Later on, the Torah relates that it took Rebecca, *whose understanding and judgment was superior to Isaac,* to discern that Jacob was the righteous son and that he, not Esau, should get the special blessing from their father.

The Talmud (Sotah 11b) asserts plainly that it was the superior moral standing of the women through which the Jews merited redemption from the slavery of Egypt.

The exodus from Egypt was the watershed upon which the entire history and development of the Jewish nation is based. And it is the women, the Talmud tells us, who were responsible for this triumph.

Not only did the women take center stage in the inauguration of the nation of Israel, but the Torah consistently credits them with responsibility for the preservation of the nation's spiritual balance.

It was the women who adamantly refused to participate in the episode of the Golden Calf.

It was the women, whose steadfast trust in God prevented them from accepting the damaging report about Israel by the Spies, and merited entry into the Land and exclusion from the death plague that befell the men of that generation.

Women Can Attain Levels of Scholarship Equal to Men

The Torah tells us about the wisdom and Torah scholarship of the daughters of Tzelophchad, and relates that they understood inheritance laws that even Moses had not known. "The daughters of Tzelophchad speak right; thou shall surely give them a possession of an inheritance among their father's brethren," said God to Moses. (Num. 27:7)

In the Book of Judges we read about Deborah, who guided the Jewish people during the era of the Judges. It was through Deborah's outstanding scholarship and spiritual guidance that the Jews overcame Yabin, the King of Canaan, who had oppressed them for many years.

In the Talmudic era we have Bruria, wife of the famous Rabbi Meir. The Talmud (Pesachim 62b) describes her extraordinary Torah scholarship by saying that Bruria studied 300 legal decisions a day.

If you understand the historical context in which these phenomena occurred, you will recognize that this is more than anecdotal lipservice to the role of women in Judaism. Women were leaders, prophetesses, and scholars in Jewish society at a time when every extant culture sacrificed women, raped them with impunity, and viewed them, at best, as chattel.

Beyond the many records of great achievements made by women, the Torah teaches us some interesting things about the essence of a woman's nature.

Rabbi Hisda explains that the word "va'yiven" (lit., "and He built") in the verse "And the Lord God built the rib" (Gen. 2:22) comes from the same root as the word "binah," understanding.

This teaches us that when God created woman from Adam's side, He gave her an added dimension of understanding, often referred to as "binah yesaira" or "women's intuition."

Woman's greater natural willingness to serve God is also borne out in the structure of Torah law, which obligates a woman in mitzvos at the age of 12, while a man is only obligated at 13. The Torah affirms that women mature more rapidly than men and are able to undertake the yoke of mitzvos at an earlier age.

Furthermore, men must perform the mitzvah of circumcision in order to enter into a convenant with God, while women become part of this covenant at birth.

Finally, a woman's natural inclination toward appreciation, understanding and trust in God make the imposition of formal catalysts toward recognition of God's existence, such as tzitzis and tefillin, entirely unnecessary and even superfluous for her.

What Is the Woman's Unique Role in Judaism?

The Torah tells us, in the story of the creation of Adam

(Gen. 1:27), that "God created the man in His own image . . . *male and female He created them.*"

The Talmud explains that Adam was originally created as an androgynous being — with both male and female characteristics. But God taught us that it was not good for the human being to be completely whole, alone, and devoted only to himself. He therefore divided Adam into two separate beings, one male and one female, making each "half" dependent on the other for completeness.

Just as God divided man and woman physically, He gave each one separate roles to play, which combine to produce spiritual completion for the couple.

Man's sphere is the external world, while woman is the instiller and protector of the vital, internal values of the Jew. The ethical, moral and spiritual personality is entrusted to the woman to create, shape and build.

This reality is reflected within Jewish law itself. Perhaps the most obvious example is the dictum that the Jewish identity of a child is determined by the mother, while the tribe is determined by the father.

Being Jewish is a reflection of the essence of the soul, and this is transmitted through the mother, who is the "caretaker" of the soul. It is the mother who determines the spiritual destiny of the child, and it is the mother who is entrusted with safeguarding the spiritual balance of the future generation. The father, on the other hand, determines the tribe to which the child belongs, which affects the physical destiny of the child. Membership in the different tribes of Israel determined which parts of the land one owned and which occupations one held.

The Centrality of the Woman's Role

The well-being of the world is dependent upon the moral, emotional and spiritual fibre of its inhabitants. It is widely recognized that healthy homes produce mature, productive members of society, while broken homes and abusive parents are more likely to produce criminals and unbalanced people. It is obvious that building a family is a role of extreme importance — a role that determines the wholesomeness or ills of our entire society.

Why then, do so many people underrate the importance of raising a family?

> In describing the importance of the woman's role in building the home, a rabbi was once challenged by a listener.
> "Well rabbi, what does *your* wife do?"
> "She's the director of a home for unwanted children," said the rabbi.
> The listener was very impressed.
> "She runs *my home*, and takes care of *my children*," added the rabbi...!

Why is it that we are impressed when someone is paid to take care of other people's children, but we are unimpressed when someone takes care of their own children?

We live in a society which evaluates the importance of everything by its price tag. Money is the primary determinant of worth. It is therefore not surprising that raising children — a no-fee position — is not viewed as worthy of respect by Western criteria.

But measuring the importance of the woman's role with the yardstick of Western values is like evaluating the worth of a painting by computing the cost of the paint and canvas. All one gets is a one-dimensional view, which does not scratch the surface of its real content.

Because society worships the external and materialistic as the epitome of achievement, it has no receptivity to spirituality, no yardstick for appreciating or measuring spiritual success. It's not that raising children has no value; it's simply that the man or woman raised in such a society has been deprived of the ability to recognize and appreciate that value.

> A man was once asked by a friend if he would lend his BMW to his housekeeper. "Of course not," the man said.
> "Why then," asked the friend, "would you entrust your *children* to her?"

Most people don't recognize the critical importance of raising children. While we can easily calculate the worth of a car, recognizing the worth of a soul requires an entirely different perspective.

At its most basic level, Judaism sees the woman as the soul and inspiration of her family. In reality, however, the sphere of a woman's influence goes far beyond.

One explanation of the verse "Ko somar l'vais Yaakov, v'sagid livnei Yisrael," is that God first addressed the women and told them about Torah observance, since the future of the nation depends on women's acceptance of Torah. They are the real power of the people. If women set their minds to keeping the Torah, then no matter what level the men are on, the women will keep the nation on course.

Rabbi Aaron Kotler, founder of the famed Beth Medrash Gevoha in Lakewood, New Jersey, once commented that it is due to the success of the Bais Yaakov women's movement, that Beth Medrash Gevoha became what it is. It was the righteous women who demanded that their husbands become Torah scholars, and that's how Beth Medrash Gevoha came into being.

Our rabbis tell us, "the final redemption from exile will come about in the merit of the righteous women."[1] Indeed, in their roles as directors of the private sphere of life, women have nothing short of the ability and opportunity to guide the very course of Jewish history.

Different But Equal

Men and women have different roles to play in Judaism. Is the role of the woman inherently inferior?

Modern society recoils at the concept of different, because it immediately sets off alarms of inferior vs. superior. It is small wonder, given the exploitation secular society has made of differences throughout history. From the oppressive treatment of the poor and landless in the caste system, to the enslavement and degradation of ethnic and racial minorities, to the horrific litany of abuse and torture in the name of "religious differences," secular society has used differences as a license to exploit those groups whom they deem "inferior."

The secular woman's experience with her differences has been equally disastrous. Women have had

---

1. Sotah 11:b

to fight fiercely to obtain basic rights — to be treated as human beings of equal worth and dignity in the home, in the workplace, and in their relationships with men. They therefore do not readily understand how they can be "different but equal," and their evaluation of Torah, in many cases, begins with the presumption that having a different role than men is categorical proof of the Torah's negative view of women.

But different does not necessarily mean inferior. Is the first baseman on a baseball team inferior to the pitcher? Is the pilot inferior to the air traffic controller? In both cases, each role is absolutely necessary for proper functioning; neither is more or less important than the other.

One of the classic examples of "different but equal" roles in the Torah, is the partnership of the tribes of Issachar and Zebulun. While Issachar was the tribe that toiled exclusively in Torah study, the tribe of Zebulun was responsible for the material support of Issachar. The Torah clearly demonstrates that the roles played in the partnership of Issachar and Zebulun produced equal spiritual merits for both.[2]

The same is true for the partnership of men and women in Judaism.

The Torah tells us, in the story of the creation of Adam (Gen. 1:27), that "God created the man in His own image... *male and female* He created them." God Himself makes it clear, through this verse, that male and female were originally created as equal parts of one whole and both of those parts are equal reflections of the "image of God."

---

2. Beraishis Rabba 99:11

After God separated woman from man, each "half" could become whole only through the unification of marriage, where man and woman become "as one flesh."

Torah Judaism assigns different roles to men and women, yet considers neither more important than the other. Both are entitled, by the mandates of Torah law, to equal respect and consideration. Both receive equal reward for the performance of their duties. But most important — both are essential to the maintenance of the Jewish home and the Jewish nation. Neither is greater than the other, because neither stands complete as an individual. Both are only parts of a greater whole. Both are only one part of the totality of what it means to be a human being.

COMMON QUESTIONS ABOUT THE WOMAN'S ROLE IN JUDAISM

Why were women given fewer mitzvos than men?

Does their exemption from "mitzvos asei she'hazman grama" (positive commandments that are dependent on time) make them inferior to men in Judaism?

The fact that women have fewer mitzvos than men does not mean that the spiritual level they can attain is inferior to that of a man. Both men and women are required to use all of their abilities to develop the closest possible relationship with God, and the potential reward awaiting each for fulfillment of their obligations is the same. Prophecy, the most intense manifestation of a relationship with God, was achieved by great women as well as great men in our history.

The difference between men and women lies in the method designed for them to achieve their common goal of "dveykus b'Hashem," and therefore in the different amount of mitzvos that devolve upon them. While women and men are enjoined equally to refrain from all "mitzvos lo saaseh" — negative prohibitions which damage a Jew's spiritual standing, women are not obligated in all of the positive mitzvos — those which actively bring a person closer to God. This is because women have a greater tendency toward spiritual growth than men and therefore do not need these mitzvos to bring that potential to fruition. They achieve it naturally.

Picture for example, two overweight people. Both are given exercise regimens by a doctor. One person has to do five hours of pushups a day, the other only two.

Which person is better off?

Obviously, the person who only needs two hours a day. Needing five hours rather than two does not make the first person more privileged. Quite the contrary. It indicates that he needs more work in order to reach his goal.

The sum total of the woman's role, however, is not simply *exemption* from time-bound mitzvos. While being exempt from those mitzvos which are not necessary for their spiritual growth, women were given three mitzvos designated especially for them; and it is primarily and preferably through the performance of these mitzvos by women that even men fulfill their obligations in these areas.

The three mitzvos given specifically to women are: kindling of the Sabbath lights, taking of Challah (portion of dough) and niddah (laws of marital separation).

It is ironic that feminists claim that women are disadvantaged by virtue of having less mitzvos, while the Torah clearly recognizes that it is precisely because they have a natural advantage in the area of spirituality that they *need* less mitzvos!

What is a woman's obligation in Torah study? What is the meaning of "Kol ha'melamed bito Torah k'ilu melamda tiflus?" ("Teaching one's daughter Torah is like teaching her triviality.")

The obligation to study Torah is a dual one. On its most practical level, it is derived from the verse, "So that you will learn them and you will observe to keep them." (Deut. 5:1).

One must study so that he will be able to perform. Torah law is extremely complex and only one who is knowledgeable can be truly observant. Women as well as men are obligated on this level, as derived from the verse in Deuteronomy (31:12),

> Assemble the people, men, women and children, and your stranger in your gates so they will hear [understand] and so that they will learn and they will fear the Lord your God and they will be cautious to perform all the words of this Torah.

The second part of the obligation concerns the constant and total intellectual involvement in all areas of Torah study, whether or not they are relevant in practice. This obligation is only binding on men, and is derived from the verse, "v'shinantam l'vanecha" — "you shall teach them to your sons." Rashi explains that the term "v'shinantam" refers to in-depth, long term study (as opposed to "essential" education for practical knowledge), and the Talmud (Kiddushin 29B) understands "l'vanecha" to mean sons, not daughters.

In other words, while women are obligated to learn a large segment of the Torah — *everything* necessary to bring about excellence in observance, love of God and fear of God — they are not required to dedicate themselves completely to a total involvement in all aspects of the word of God. This is because they were given a monumental assignment — the care of their family — which takes up a large part of their time and energy. It is obvious that if women were commanded as were men, to dedicate all of their abilities, energies and time to every area of Torah study, they would not be in a position to carry out their family responsibilities.

This does not mean that a woman who is either free of those responsibilities or who feels a strong desire to study additional areas of Torah not related to her observance is *prohibited* from doing so. She is certainly permitted to do so, and moreover, receives reward for such study.

However, the rabbis strongly caution that casual study of Torah — particularly Talmud, which takes a great deal of dedication and long-term commitment — is at best unproductive and at worst misleading.

This is what the rabbis meant when they said that teaching Torah to women is teaching them "tiflus" (triviality). Since the amount of time and attention most women would have to give to the less relevant areas of Torah study is relatively small, the possibility of these areas being studied incompletely is very great. It is therefore preferable that they do not start an endeavor to which they cannot give proper attention. That is why they are exempt (exempt, not *excluded*) from such study. This is in no way a slight to their intelligence. It is rather a recognition of the importance of their primary responsibility.

Why can't a woman be a witness?

Which position within the Jewish nation requires greater intellectual capacity and integrity: a witness or a *leader*?

Clearly, a leader needs the keener intellectual faculties. *Deborah (Judg. 4:4)* was a prime example of a woman who merited becoming the leader and judge of the nation. It is obvious, then, that the disqualification of women as witnesses has nothing to do with intellectual stability or personal credibility.

Tanna de bei Eliyahu asks: "What was so special about Deborah that she deserved to be a judge and a prophetess in Israel? Was not Pinchas, son of Elazar alive yet (and therefore more deserving to assume such a high position)?

> But I call upon heaven and earth to witness, be it a gentile or a Jew, a man or a woman, a manservant or a maidservant, the spirit of God rests upon an individual only according to his deeds.

It is illuminating to realize that while secular society has only relatively recently awarded women the right to vote, ancient Israel's highest positions were available to women from the very start!

The Talmud tells us that disqualification as a witness can be based upon one of two different factors: technical disqualification or credibility disqualification.

Listed among those who are disqualified based upon *technical considerations* are relatives of a defendant, someone who would have to give testimony against himself, kings of Israel — and women.

For purposes of accusation, Jewish law requires testimony by two eyewitnesses, free of all technical disqualifications. Therefore, in these cases, women may not give testimony.

However, for purposes of identification, where credible statements are needed, a woman's statement is fully accepted.

In ritual matters, for example, such as kashrus or family purity, we rely equally on statements of women and men in determining the facts.

Furthermore, oaths are administered only to persons with credibility. While they are not taken by gamblers, usurers, insane persons, or minors, oaths are administered in court to men and women alike.

So why are women technically disqualified to testify in certain areas of witnessed testimony? Like many other aspects of Jewish law, this might be understood, simply, as a heavenly decree; or it might be seen as having deeper implications.

A king is disqualified from being a witness (see Rambam, Hilchos Melachim 3:7). Illustrious kings of Israel — even David and Solomon — were not permitted to testify; the reason is that the adversarial attitude of the court to a witness and the respect and deference due a king are mutually exclusive.

In a similar vein, one explanation of why a woman cannot be a witness is that it would be contradictory to the basic principles of the private role of women in Jewish life to require them to testify at all times. As has been stated, "The entire glory of the daughter of a king lies on the inside." Women, therefore, are even exempt from the requirement that a litigant must appear himself in a court, rather than appoint an attorney to appear in his stead.[1]

Thus we learn that women retain equal credibility with men; their oath is fully acceptable in court, as is the oath of any credible individual. However, women are disqualified from the obligation to testify only where witnessed testimony is required.

Why do men make the blessing, "Shelo asani isha" ("...that You have not made me a woman") in their daily prayers?

Why do women make the blessing "She'asani kirtzono" ("...that I was made according to God's will")?

There are few prohibitions in the Torah that are of greater severity than speaking ill of another person. The sin of Loshon Hora carries with it numerous prohibitions and, according to our rabbis, is in some ways worse than even the three cardinal sins for which a Jew must give up his life rather than transgress.

It becomes quite clear then, that the blessing "Shelo Asani Isha" can in no way be intended to derogate women. Men cannot be commanded to get up every

---

1. Talmud Shevuos 30a and the Tosfos there; Gittin 41a; Kesubos 74b

morning and slander women. What then, is its meaning?

One explanation of the meaning of the blessing "Shelo Asani Isha" is that it is an expression of man's gratitude to God that he was created spiritually inferior to women and therefore must work harder to *earn* completion. This extra work required of man accords him greater pleasure — if he successfully attains it — than if he had been born with the woman's natural inclination to serve God.[2]

Let us return to the earlier example of two overweight people who each require a different exercise regimen. The person who has to lose a large amount of weight and does so successfully will take a greater pleasure in his new physique than would someone who only had to work a little to achieve it.

On the other hand, it can be said that women, in recognition of their elevated spiritual capacity, make the blessing "She'asani Kirtzono," acknowledging that they are starting out naturally closer to the "ratzon Hashem," to fulfilling the will of God.

Chazal tell us that the description of man as an "Ish," as opposed to "Adam," indicates that he is a tzaddik. [We know that the meraglim (spies) were all great men because the Torah refers to them as "Ish."]

Man's blessing is said in the negative (*she'lo asani*) because, unlike woman, he cannot make a blessing on that which may not yet exist. His status as an "Ish" is something he spends his life trying to attain. But since

---

2. The Torah relates a similar concept when it compares angels to human beings. The pleasure that a human being can attain is greater than that which an angel can achieve because a human being's level of spirituality is earned, while an angel is given it.

it is not a given, Chazal cannot phrase his blessing as a positive affirmation of his status as an Ish.

Women, on the other hand, achieve their status as an Isha from birth, and can definitively say, "She'asani Kirtzono."

Why can't a woman be part of a minyan?

As was explained earlier, the man was given the public role in Judaism, while the inner role, the private sector, was assigned to the woman.

A minyan is a public unit, expressive of the public functioning of the community. Therefore only men, as the public figures, can legally form a minyan. While women may participate in public prayer, they cannot be one of the ten that make up a minyan, since women are responsible for developing the area of private responsibility and therefore always remain ten private individuals, rather than a unit of ten members.[3]

Why can't a woman lead the prayers?

There is a general rule that only a person who is under obligation to do a particular mitzvah can perform that mitzvah for others who are also under obligation. For example, if one eats bread and is required to make a blessing, he can at the same time discharge someone else of his duty to make the blessing. But if one does not eat bread and thus is not required to make a blessing himself, he cannot discharge someone who is about to eat bread and is *obligated* to make a blessing.

---

3. Rosh Hashanah 29a.

Similarly, since women are not required to participate in communal prayer, they cannot act on behalf of the community in prayer. The duty of the chazan is to be the emissary of the community and act in its behalf. Women, owing to their more private obligation, are not required to participate in communal prayer and therefore cannot act as emissaries of those who are.[4]

Why can't a woman inherit?

This is a law cited by many feminists in an attempt to make their case that the Torah is biased against women. However, an understanding of the laws of inheritance will demonstrate that this law is actually a protection for the rights of woman, rather than a hindrance to them.

Under Jewish law, the heirs to a man's estate may not claim their inheritance until all creditors have been satisfied.

Because the Torah wanted to insure that the woman and daughters would be guaranteed continuing support from the estate of the deceased, it designated the wife and daughters as *creditors*, as opposed to heirs.[5] They therefore have a lien on all the decedent's property, which has priority over all heirs and, furthermore, precedes all creditors subsequent to her marriage.

The Torah did not want to compel a woman, who may not have been prepared to earn a living, to do so in

---

4. Ibid.
5. Maimonides, Ishut 17:1-8; Bava Basra 175b, 176a

the event of a death of her spouse. Therefore it gave her the favored status of creditor. The sons, on the other hand, receive only that which is left after the claims of the woman and daughters have been satisfied. In the event that there is only enough money to support the wife and daughters, the sons must find other ways to support themselves.

A father is fully entitled to give his daughter a gift of any portion of his estate. Since the sons, as inheritors, have no lien on the property, their inheritance rights do not limit the father's ability to give his daughters a gift.

Thus, in making the wife and daughters creditors instead of heirs, the Torah provided for the maximum possible support of the wife and daughters!

Why does Jewish law require a married woman to cover her hair?

Central to the Jewish marriage is the concept of sep-arateness from others — *kedushin.* A husband and wife are consecrated solely to each other and their relationship is intensely private, separate and qualita-tively different than their relationships with any other person.

Among the forms that this separateness and pri-vacy takes is in the realm of sexuality. The physical relationship between husband and wife is uncondi-tionally private and exclusive. While a married woman should certainly present a neat and attractive image to the world, she must protect the privacy of her relation-ship with her husband by dressing in a manner that is not alluring or seductive to others. This is the reason why a married woman covers her hair. A significant part of a woman's sexual allure is her hair. In covering it, the woman reserves this aspect of her beauty solely for her husband and heightens the degree of intimacy and attraction that they alone share.

Does the status of being "tamay" imply spiritual inferiority?

One problem that causes difficulty when people begin to learn about various concepts in Judaism is the translation of Hebrew words. Many of these words have no precise English definition because they express spiritual ideas that have no parallel in English culture.

Such is the case with the words "Tahara" and "Tuma."

These words are popularly translated into English as "purity" and "impurity."

Herein lies the gist of the problem.

In the English language, the word "pure" implies something perfectly clean, flawless, unpolluted or innocent.

A quick check of the word "impure" in your thesaurus will yield synonyms such as "contaminated," "corrupt," "tainted," and "unclean."

Take, for example, the advertisement slogan for a bar of Ivory Soap: "99.44% pure." The implication is that Ivory Soap is a nearly perfect product. It contains only a tiny percentage of undesirable ingredients.

That is why so many people think that "Tamay" means "spiritually undesirable" or "dirty."

And that is why so many women believe that the laws of Nida and the halachic condition of "Tuma," are a clear manifestation of the negative attitude the Torah has toward women and their "denegrated" status when they are a Nida.

This feeling, coupled with the belief that "Tuma" applies *only* to women and sexuality, creates the impression that women are discriminated against in Judaism, and that sexuality is considered "dirty."

Nothing could be further from the truth.

The English concepts of "pure" and "impure" are completely unrelated to the Jewish concepts of Tuma and Tahara.

The way to rectify the misconception is to first explain that the words "Tuma" and "Tahara" are spiritual concepts that *have no translation or parallel* in the English language. Do not attempt to find a one-word definition.

Explain the *entire concept* as it exists in Judaism:

The central tenet of Judaism is that God is one. Absolutely one. There is no force that exists independent of Him.

Man's struggle in this world — the exercise of his free will — is in choosing either to move toward God and reality, or to move away from God, to illusion or nothingness.

We call these choices "good" and "evil." When man makes a choice that moves him closer to God, he is choosing "good." When he makes a choice that moves him away from God, he is choosing "evil."[6]

Evil has no intrinsic reality. It is the absence of good, or the absence of an open manifestation of God. God's existence can be open and clear to us, or it can be hidden from us.

---

6. Rambam, Moreh Nevuchim, Part 3, Chapt. 23

The open presence of God is what we call "Tahara."
A state of God's hiddenness is what we call "Tuma."

In other words, "Tuma" is really a "Tahara-vaccum."

The state of Tuma can devolve upon men, women and animals. When the open presence of God — the neshama, or life — leaves a man, woman or animal, that body becomes Tamay.

The highest "Tahara-vaccum" is a dead body.

Let's go back, for a moment, to the English concept of "Tuma" as "spiritually undesirable" or "dirty."

Which would you think is more "spiritually unclean" — a dead dog or a dead human being?

Most people would think a dog is more "spiritually unclean" because it is a lower form of existence than a human being.

Wrong.

The dead body of a human being contains a much greater degree of "Tuma."

Why?

Because the human being, when it is alive and filled with a neshama — the open manifestation of God's presence — has a much greater condition of Tahara. The manifestation of Godliness within a human being is far greater than that within an animal. Therefore, when the neshama departs, it leaves behind a much greater vacuum of Tahara, a much stronger Tuma, than that of an animal.

Next in the ranks of "Tuma" is a Yoledes: a woman who gives birth. The reason she is Tamay is because a degree of spiritual vacuum is created by the departure of the extra life within her — the child.

It is interesting that when a woman gives birth to a girl, her state of "Tuma" is twice that of when she gives birth to a boy. That is because the presence of a female child within her gives her a greater state of "Tahara." The female bears within her the power to give life, a condition that is an open manifestation of Godliness, and a higher level of "Tahara." The departure of a female child, therefore, is the departure of a creation with a higher level of "Tahara" than a male child. This departure creates a greater spiritual vacuum. Hence, the Yoledes is Tamay for a longer period of time.

Following the departure of life itself, among the degrees of Tuma, is the loss of "potential life."

This Tuma affects both men and women.

After having relations, men are in a state of Tuma, because of the loss of the "building blocks" of life within them. And women incur this state of Tuma when they menstruate, because of the loss of potential life within them.

In sum, Tuma is a concept which describes a loss of life or spirituality. It is not a description of spiritual inferiority, impurity or uncleanliness.

Note: In an effort to give the student a grasp of a Jewish concept, we often supply an English word that captures some of the meaning, but not all of it. In doing so, we cause the student to misunderstand the concept altogether, or to assign the additional, unrelated associations in the English word to the Hebrew idea, distorting it entirely.

One common example of this is in connection with the laws of Shabbos: the definition of the word "Melacha." The most popular English translation of this word is "work." Translating "Melacha" as "work" gives the student the impression that any activity that requires heavy physical exertion is proscribed on Shabbos and, conversely, something that takes little or no effort is permitted. Consequently, explaining why flicking on a light switch is "work" becomes extremely difficult. Once the concept of "physical work" is firmly set in the student's mind, he will not understand why taking an elevator should be forbidden on Shabbos, while trekking up ten flights of stairs is permitted.

Certain Jewish concepts, when translated in English, create even bigger problems. Not only is the concept conveyed inaccurately, but the English word comes with its own "baggage" that does not apply to the Hebrew word and gives the Hebrew word a pejorative connotation that is absolutely false. This is the case with Tuma and Tahara, as explained above.

Therefore, wherever possible, avoid translating Hebrew words describing spiritual concepts. Instead, *transliterate* them. Then give the student a clear and complete explanation of the idea. This way, the student will absorb the Hebrew word as a new addition to his vocabulary instead of viewing it as a synonym for an existing English word and applying inappropriate interpretations to the concept.

SUFFERING

Empathy is Often More Important Than Logic

The question of why God allows pain and suffering to exist in the world is something which troubles many people. It is one of the key issues confronted when people begin to formulate ideas about Judaism. And it is often the first question to arise when people contemplate a personal or national trauma, whether it be sickness, injury, death, or the Holocaust. Without suitable responses to their questions, people could be more inclined to reject or ignore God, than to try to understand Him.

Keep in mind that any discussion of suffering could become highly emotional and volatile. You must be sensitive to the fact that some of the people who confront you with this question may be grappling with their own profoundly painful events. In these instances, carefully evaluate if the person is seeking an intellectual answer to his question or a simple show of empathy for what he has endured. Logical solutions will not help someone in need of support and concern. If the person is not in search of real answers, your explanations will have little impact, no matter how correct they may be.

Most People Accept the Jewish Concept of God

When people attempt to reconcile the phenomenon of

suffering of the innocent with the notion of a just and caring God, they often come to the conclusion that the two cannot exist together: that suffering, in and of itself, *disproves* the existence of God.

However, there is a logical error in this reasoning.

What if, theoretically, God is not just? In that case, suffering would pose no contradiction to His existence.

To the skeptic, suffering might, at best, disprove the existence of a *just* God. It is not, in any way, proof that there is *no* God.

Why do people rarely conclude that God is not just? What causes them instead to deny the possibility of God altogether?

Interestingly, most people intuitively accept the Jewish concept that God, *by definition*, is just. Therefore, if there is no justice, there can be no God. The existence of "unjust suffering" does not cause people to revise their understanding of God. They simply conclude that there must be no God at all.

Paradoxically, it is only because they believe in the Jewish concept of a perfect, just God, that they have a question about suffering in the first place!

Keep in mind that this is only a starting point with which to begin the discussion. It is not an explanation of how Judaism views the existence of a perfectly just God despite perceived injustice in this world. It is simply presented here to demonstrate that the questioner has subconsciously accepted the Jewish point of view from the outset.

Finding the Meaning in Suffering

It is important to pinpoint the exact problem bothering

the questioner. People often assume that the basic existence of suffering in the world is what causes the difficulty. Although it is legitimate to ask the existential question of why a loving God would create a world with suffering in it, this is not usually what causes distress. More often than not, the questions are caused by what appears to be *unfair*, or *meaningless* suffering. In other words, why does God appear to allow or cause "unjust" suffering?

People have often endured suffering without questioning God's justice, as long as they understood the goal toward which their suffering was directed and believed it worthwhile. Childbirth is a classic example. Millions of women willingly endure the wrenching pains of labor in order to bear a child. Very few question the existence of God when they are holding their newborn. Despite the pain they underwent, the gift of life is of immense significance, and because they understand that so clearly, they do not question the justness of the suffering in that experience.

This, incidentally, is why the metaphor of "labor and childbirth" is so often used to describe the travails of the Jewish people in the diaspora.[1] Like the pains of childbirth, the indescribable sufferings of our nation intermingle with an optimism arising from the certainty that lasting goodness will ultimately come from this pain; that our suffering is not in vain.

What plagues most people, however, is the perception that the pain or suffering they are experiencing is *not* leading toward any worthwhile purpose and is therefore "unjust." It is this perception that leads them to wonder about God's justice and/or His existence.

---

1. Kesuvos 111; Sanhedrin 98B

To illustrate, compare the following situations.

Imagine a family whose son has died in the recent Persian Gulf War. In a heroic attempt to save the lives of his friends and fellow soldiers, this young man dove onto a live grenade, and sacrificed his own life in the process.

What is the reaction of the family? Shock and pain, of course, at the loss of their son. But also intense pride in their son's heroism. Since they can see the *meaningfulness* behind their son's death, their knee-jerk response is not, "Where was God?" Rather, they view his sacrifice as noble and worthwhile and therefore generally do not come to question God's justice or His existence.

Now imagine if the same family's five-year old son had been tragically run over by a hit-and-run driver while playing outside his house. In this case, we would expect to hear questions about why such a tragedy could take place in the face of a just and loving God. Why? Because, in this case, the benefit and purpose of this child's death is not at all clear.

This concept is also true in the case of large-scale tragedies. For example, if you ask most people if they were and are still in favor of the establishment of the State of Israel, most people would respond positively, despite the loss of life entailed in creating the State of Israel, and in preserving it. In the short 44-year history of the modern State of Israel, close to 10,000 Jewish lives have been sacrificed. Yet, to most Jews, the existence of a national homeland for the Jewish people is justifiable and worthwhile enough to warrant the cost involved.

Therefore, one way to reconcile suffering with the existence of a just God, is to understand the purpose

that makes the pain worthwhile. When we do understand the value and benefit that comes as a result of
our pain, we accept it in most cases as just.

If you can teach someone to try to understand,
even partially, what his personal suffering may have
accomplished, such as self-growth and an improved
appreciation of the value of life, it is likely that he will
be more able to come to grips with the painful event
and maintain his awareness of God's goodness and
justness.

Viktor Frankl, a noted psychotherapist who in-
vented a school of psychotherapy called logotherapy,
based his techniques on the concept that helping people find meaning in their lives or in an experience of
suffering will enable them to cope with *any* difficulty
in a healthy, stable way.

The following passages from Frankl's famous work,
Man's Search for Meaning, illustrate this point.

> *Once an elderly general practitioner consulted me be-*
> *cause of his severe depression. He could not overcome*
> *the loss of his wife who had died two years before and*
> *whom he had loved above all else. Now, how could I*
> *help him? What should I tell him? Well, I refrained from*
> *telling him anything but instead confronted him with*
> *the question, 'What would have happened, Doctor, if*
> *you had died first, and your wife would have had*
> *to survive you?' 'Oh,' he said, 'for her this would*
> *have been terrible; how she would have suffered!'*
> *Whereupon I replied, 'You see, Doctor, such a suffering*
> *has been spared her, and it was you who have spared*
> *her this suffering — to be sure, at the price that now*
> *you have to survive and mourn her.' He said no word*
> *but shook my hand and calmly left my office. In some*

way, suffering ceases to be suffering at the moment it finds a meaning, such as the meaning of sacrifice.

Of course, this was no therapy in the proper sense, since, first, his despair was no disease; and second, I could not change his fate; I could not revive his wife. But in that moment I did succeed in changing his attitude toward his unalterable fate inasmuch as from that time on he could at least see a meaning in his suffering. It is one of the basic tenets of logotherapy that man's main concern is not to gain pleasure or to avoid pain but rather to see a meaning in his life. That is why man is even ready to suffer, on the condition, to be sure, that his suffering has a meaning....

In another exchange,

...a rabbi from Eastern Europe turned to me and told me his story. He had lost his first wife and their six children in the concentration camp of Auschwitz where they were gassed, and now it turned out that his second wife was sterile. I observed that procreation is not the only meaning of life, for then life in itself would become meaningless, and something which in itself is meaningless cannot be rendered meaningful merely by its perpetuation. However, the rabbi evaluated his plight as an Orthodox Jew in terms of despair that there was no son of his own who would ever say Kaddish for him after his death.

But I would not give up. I made a last attempt to help him by inquiring whether he did not hope to see his children again in Heaven. However, my question was followed by an outburst of tears, and now the true reason for his despair came to the fore: he explained that his children, since they died as innocent martyrs, were thus found worthy of the highest place in Heaven, but as for himself he could not expect, as

*an old, sinful man, to be assigned the same place. I did
not give up but retorted, 'Is it not conceivable, Rabbi,
that precisely this was the meaning of your surviving
your children: that you may be purified through these
years of suffering, so that finally you, too, though not
innocent like your children, may become worthy of
joining them in Heaven? Is it not written in the Psalms
that God preserves all your tears? So perhaps none
of your sufferings were in vain.' For the first time in
many years he found relief from his suffering through
the new point of view which I was able to open up to
him.*

God Loves Us Like a Parent Loves His Child

Rabbi Zecharya Graineman, ztz'l, in a discussion with
Aish HaTorah students, stated that his first bout with
cancer spurred him to grow to levels he had not previously been able to attain. He added that, given the
choice, he would still rather have had the cancer than
not.

Rabbi Graineman was an unusually strong and
perceptive man. Most people do not have such a keen
awareness of the meaning and purpose of life, even
when their lives are proceeding without major discom-
fort. Certainly, they could not be expected to effort-
lessly tune out the pain and suffering of a personal or-
deal and focus solely on the benefit of it. Nevertheless,
regardless of one's reaction to suffering, the Torah tells
us, "Just as a man chastises his son, God your Lord
chastises you."[2] A loving parent punishes the child *for*

---

2. Devarim 8:5

the child's own good, and preferably in way that allows the child to grasp the purpose of the punishment and understand how to change. God's punishment is likewise for our betterment and is administered in a way that, with introspection and reflection, is often accessible to our understanding.

Why is it that people do not always perceive this so readily? Because we have a limited understanding of reality and of ourselves. Anyone who has ever taken their young child to the doctor to be innoculated, understands this immediately. Try explaining to your two-year old that the four-inch needle the doctor is about to insert in her arm is for her own good. Even though you know it is, she does not have the maturity and perspective to be able to see it as such.

The same is true between man and God, but in much greater proportions. In the headiness of incredible technological and scientific achievement, mankind has come to assume that everything is attainable and understandable. We have forgotten that our understanding is not necessarily the infallible arbiter of good and bad.

Human beings are bound by time, space and a finite mind. We are only privy to a tiny slice of reality which is far from the whole picture. God's infinite perspective encompasses the entire span of history and every aspect of existence.

Recognition of our limited understanding of God's Divine Plan is implied in the blessing we make upon receiving bad news: "Baruch Dayan Ha'Emes." ("Blessed is the Truthful Judge") In this world, the only way we can respond to events that appear to us as "bad" is to strengthen our understanding that God is indeed just and that this event is somehow for our benefit.

However, in the World to Come, says the Talmud[3], when we will have perfect clarity, we will be able to recite the joyous blessing "Baruch HaTov V'HaMaytiv" ("Blessed is He Who Is Good and Who Does Good") on both the good *and* bad things that have happened throughout history. Our clarity will be so keen that we will be able to perceive the absolute goodness and meaning in seemingly "bad" events and make a blessing over them with equal gratitude and happiness.

We must therefore try to teach people, through an objective, broad-based view of life, that *everything* God does is for our welfare. (See essay, "The Gift of Life," at the end of this section, for a fuller presentation of this concept.) One must judge God, not through the prism of *one event*, but through the composite mosaic of every experience God has designed for our lives. Without that perspective, any evaluation of God will be skewed, and conclusions reached will necessarily be flawed. Within that context, even when one does not instinctively recognize the purpose of a particular event, the simple understanding that the source is God will instill the confidence that it, too, is somehow for his benefit.

This, in fact, is the theme behind Kaddish. Chazal understood that a mourner's deepest need is to clarify that God is just and that all His ways are righteous and good. The words of Kaddish, which acknowledge God's sovereignty over the world and signify that everything happens for a Divine Purpose, enable the mourner to cope with his pain, fortified with the knowledge that life and death are meaningful and that he is not a victim of "simple bad luck."

---

3. Pesachim 50

In summary, it would obviously be very convenient if we could instantly perceive the benefits that life's difficulties and challenges bring to our lives. However, in many situations that is unlikely to be the case. On occasions where the value or benefit of the suffering is not clear, we must stimulate our awareness of how much God has given us in order to reinforce our perception of His love for us. We must each try to reconnect to a time in our lives when we truly felt God to be our Father in Heaven. Awakening those emotions will help build the understanding that every event in life is a reflection of God's goodness and is designed for our ultimate benefit.

The Gift of Life: An Essay

It's 6:30 a.m. The alarm clock goes off. Ilana stirs and takes for granted the enjoyment of feeling alive in the morning with all her limbs intact and body systems in perfect working order. She reaches across her night-table, turns off the alarm and switches on the radio. She then grumpily pulls herself out of bed and into the bathroom. The splash of water on her face feels pretty good in the morning and the hot shower even better. By the time she dresses, the half-asleep grump of just half an hour ago is smiling at what she sees in the mirror (she always thought that blouse looked kind of spiffy).

The crunch of the cereal and its nutty flavor, followed by the first cup of great smelling, brewed coffee really has her going now. Before she boards the train for the 45 minute commute to work she grabs the morning paper and on this particular day manages to claim a window seat. The passing scenery is charming and captivating. Ilana remembers her weekend spent in the country and smiles at how quickly the time passed in the company of her sister, brother-in-law and their children.

Her stop comes up and she breaks from her reverie to bolt for the train door, up the stairs and escalator, and through the door of her tiny office on the 34th floor in her city's central mid-town location. Gazing at her calendar she notes a lighter than usual workday and immediately pencils in a one-hour lunch she's planning to do solo near the park.

Returning yesterday's unreturned phone calls, Ilana manages to tidy up two rather difficult previously unresolved issues and to turn a decent profit on what she thought was a lost opportunity. It was a good, solid morning, she mused to herself over a still warm take-out lunch, as she looked out across acres of unbroken rows of trees and greens.

The rest of her workday was more frenetically paced, with minor and major problems unfolding at the rate of about three an hour. Still, after a couple of calls where she had to raise her voice and one unpleasant run-in with an anti-social superior, her day is done. Glancing at tomorrow's calendar she allows herself a grunt of satisfaction at having handled all the curves thrown her that day with style and aplomb.

Moments later she finds herself on the indoor tennis court swinging her racket deftly and accurately to easily defeat her good friend and athletically superior opponent. Coming home to her neat apartment, she relaxes with a good book and a small glass of wine and after the required call to her folks, turns out the lights and floats off to sleep.

Hardly a remarkable day? Perhaps, but let's take a moment to review and examine her pleasures on this mundane, nondescript day.

Like most people, our central character misses out on more pleasure than she actually enjoys, simply because she hasn't learned to focus on them. The pleasures of awakening in the morning and feeling rested, alive, empowered as a thinking human, the renewed functioning of each limb, the restoration of sight to the eyes, the ability to balance and coordinate to get out of bed, etc. seem to have passed her by.

But she does enjoy the splash of cold water on her sleepy face, the invigorating hot water raining down from the shower, her ability to choose, match and wear well coordinated clothing, the simple pleasure of the breakfast biscuit and sip of fresh coffee, the quick update on world and local events, reliving the memories of playing with her cooing niece and of chasing and being chased through country fields by her toddler nephews, the accomplishment of conducting herself well in the face of competition and adversity, the delightful lunch by the park, concluding her day with a feeling of accomplishment and topping it of with hard play and relaxation.

In short, although the day could have been even better, there was pleasure to be derived in just about every part of it.

If basic monotheism teaches us that these pleasures weren't just happenstance — but were prepared for us by the Almighty, who bestowed us with each one as a gift, — then every single one becomes significant and even more pleasurable.

It would seem that her entire life was made for pleasure. Of course there are challenges and disappointments, but simply experiencing life holds the potential for a great deal of joy and pleasure.

Imagine now that she is awakened by a call in the middle of the night. The news is terrible. Her father has succumbed to a combination of heart disease and asthma. He was just 62 and was the kindest and most wonderful person anyone could be.

Sobbing, she places the receiver back in its cradle, thinking about the injustice of it all. "God how could you take my Dad this way, when he never even hurt a fly?"

Suddenly God has acted unjustly. Interestingly, God hasn't entered the picture until now. Had she paused at each of her pleasures to realize that they were engineered by God specifically for her enjoyment, she perhaps would have realized, too, that her father's death at the hands of the same Creator, far from being a meaningless occurrence, is just and holds a great deal of significance to her and to all those who knew her father.

Ironically, the propensity to blame God for the bad news is in itself a tacit admission that it is God who is in charge. How unfortunate that the daily megadose of pleasures available to us — each of which points to God's purpose for creation — are all but ignored, while upon witnessing death and suffering we readily label God "the Terminator."

However, by taking one or two steps back and stopping to smell the roses, it becomes clear that there is great joy to be experienced in life by recognizing its inherent pleasures and knowing who our Benefactor is. The agony and pain associated with suffering are, in fact, exacerbated by ignoring the purpose of Creation and the meaning of the life. This tends to leave us feeling like a pin-ball, bouncing wildly, randomly and out-of-control off of each of life's switches, bells and buzzers.

Examining the genius of creation, the perfection of balanced eco-systems, the robotic and computational wizardry of the human body and mind, and the sheer delight available in just living, one can't help but notice creative brilliance and intricate purpose. In both the good times and the bad.

GOD'S FOREKNOWLEDGE AND OUR FREE WILL

If God knows the future, how is it possible for human beings to have free will?

When we look back in history to a particular event, our knowledge of what took place at that time does not in any way limit the choices of the people who actually participated in that event. They had complete freedom to choose as they did. We are merely aware of what they chose.

For example, the fact that we know that John F. Kennedy chose to ride in a motorcade in Dallas on November 22, 1963 and was subsequently shot, does not interfere with his free will to have chosen that course of action.

However human beings cannot know the future. Therefore, if we do know exactly what someone is going to do in a future situation, it must mean that the person had only one fixed option in that situation. In other words, "Person A"'s foreknowledge of "Person B"'s actions makes it logically impossible for "Person B" to have complete freedom of choice.

However, God's nature differs from man's in a way that eliminates the contradiction between foreknowledge and free will.

For God exists outside of time. The past, present and future always exist concurrently for Him. Therefore, God can always "look back" at our choices without affecting them. Even our future choices can be viewed by God in retrospect — because 100 years ago, today, and 100 years from now exist simultaneously before God. Therefore, God's knowledge of what we have chosen, presently choose or will choose is not an impediment to our free will.

Age OF THE UNIVERSE

Scientific dating methods estimate that the universe is billions of years old. To most secular Jews, these findings constitute a clear contradiction to the Torah point of view and are often a license to discredit the validity of Torah. However, this contradiction is simply a result of the erroneous perception that the Torah claim is that the world was created exactly 5,753 years and six days ago. In order to eliminate the contradiction, you must correct this misunderstanding.

According to the Torah, the world is 5,753 years and six *time periods* old. The word used by the Torah to refer to these time periods is "Yom," which is, for lack of a better word, loosely translated as "day." When the Torah says that the world was created in six "Yoms," many commentaries understand that the word "Yom" is not the same as a 24 hour day.[1]

Our "day" is defined as one rotation of the earth upon its axis. A "Yom," on the other hand, is defined as a period of light and dark. Today, with every rotation of the earth upon its axis, any point on earth alternates between facing the sun and receiving light and facing away from the sun and not receiving any light. Therefore, today a "Yom," which is a period of light and dark, occurs within a twenty-four hour day.

---

1. See Sforno and Akaydas Yitzchok on length of "Yom." (Beraishis 1:5) Also see Ramban in his disputation at Barcelona on the meaning of "Yom" — not a day, but a period of time. See Rav Hirsch and Malbim on "Or" as opposed to "M'or."

However, this could not have been the case immediately after Creation, because *the sun was not formed until the fourth "Yom."* Therefore, the period of dark and light called "Yom" in the Torah's account of the first four days of creation has nothing to do with our concept of the twenty-four hour day, which is the period of light and darkness produced by the earth's rotation toward and away from the sun.

As Torah Jews, we have always understood that the age of the universe is 5,753 years *plus* an indeterminate period of time called six "Yom." We certainly do not know the length of a "Yom" during the first four days of creation. It could have been billions of years. The discovery by physicists and cosmologists that the world is billions of years old in no way contradicts the Torah's account of creation.

Our calendar begins with the creation of the first man, Adam, who was created exactly 5,753 years ago. The fact that many years could have elapsed in the period before Adam's creation is something Judaism has always recognized.

Note: There are many other approaches one may use to reconcile the apparent contradiction between the Jewish calendar system and the dating methods used by scientists. The above explanation was chosen simply because we felt it would be the most practical one to deliver.

THE THEORY OF EVOLUTION

Most secular Jews are acquainted with the theory of evolution and have accepted it, at least in part, as a legitimate explanation for the origin of life.

We have found that it is generally unproductive to dismiss the theory of evolution as erroneous. First of all, most of us do not have a sufficiently thorough understanding of the theory to expose all of its mathematical and scientific flaws. Second, discrediting the theory of evolution causes the secular Jew to believe that he must disregard science and reason in order to be a Torah Jew.

Instead, if we give evolutionary theory some credibility as a mechanism of creation, the secular Jew will not be forced to abandon a theory which he feels has been substantiated by science. We can accomplish this by demonstrating that, as many of our sages explain, it is possible from a Torah perspective to accept the notion that the world was formed by God through an evolutionary process.

Rashi comments on the verse "Let the earth bring forth living animals," (Genesis 1:24) that "All were created on the first day and there remained only to *draw them out.*" In other words, God created everything *in potential* on day one, and the different species He designed "evolved" on subsequent days from that which was created on the first day. Rashi makes this point several times, in his comments on Verses 14 and 24 in Chapter 1 of Genesis, and on Verse 4 in Chapter 2.

Maimonides makes this point as well. In *Guide for the Perplexed*, he explains creation as follows: *"Everything was created simultaneously; then gradually all things became differentiated.* They have compared this to what happens when an agricultural laborer sows various kinds of grain in the soil at the same moment. Some of them sprout within a day, others within two days, others again within three days, though everything was sowed at the same hour."

The claim made by evolutionists that the earth evolved through a process in which more complex organisms emerged from simpler ones, is a view espoused by many Torah sages. However, we differ with evolutionists who claim that all of this could have occurred randomly. In fact, many scientists also reject the possibility of organisms having arisen randomly through evolution.[1]

Moreover, Darwin himself never believed that life could have evolved randomly. In *The Origin of the Species*, (6th edition, p. 242) Darwin writes,

> He who believes that some ancient form was transformed suddenly through an internal force or tendency ... will further be compelled to believe that many structures beautifully adapted to all the other parts of the same creature and to the surrounding conditions, have been suddenly produced; and of such complex and wonderful co-adaptations, he will not be able to assign a shadow of an explanation...

---

1. In point of fact, even according to scientists, the concept of randomness is difficult to support. The odds of even a single, viable bacterium evolving by chance on earth are too infinitesimal to bear intelligent consideration. For a more detailed explanation of the development of evolution theory, please refer to the Appendix.

To admit all this is, as it seems to me, to enter into
the realms of miracle, and to leave those of Science."

Rashi and Maimonides, who both maintained that
God created the world with an evolutionary mechanism, lived in the 11th and 12th centuries, long before
Darwin's publishing of *Origin of the Species*. Darwin's
theory of evolution, therefore, was part of our Sage's
traditional understanding of the Torah's account of
creation.

Postscript

The question of whether G-d created the world or
whether it emerged as an accident could serve as a
springboard for discussion about the nature of man
and how he differs from an animal.

If the world was produced by a random explosion
of chemicals, then human beings are simply more
intelligent creatures than animals. In that case, we
would have no reason to treat people better than we
treat animals, unless we believe that being smarter
entitles us to better treatment. According to that logic,
one could justify eating a severely retarded person or
someone in a coma, while treating bright dolphins with
greater concern.

Why is that most people feel that human beings are
entitled to greater concern than animals?

Ask even the strictest vegetarian, "If you were confronted with a situation in which the only way to save
children's lives would be to develop medicine that is
derived by killing animals, would you feel this was
justified or would you let the children die?"

If people are only smarter animals, how do we justify the difference in the way we treat them?

Furthermore, if a human being is only a smarter animal, there would be no reason to expect better moral behavior of him than we expect of an animal. When sharks eat people, we don't condemn them as being immoral; we accept the fact that they are only doing what sharks do.

Do we react the same way when one human being kills another?

Clearly, we all know instinctively that there is something in man which makes him qualitatively superior to the animal. That "something" is a soul.

How to Teach

ON BEING A CHAVRUSA (STUDY PARTNER)

YOUR GOALS:

Your goal as a chavrusa is to try to facilitate the spiritual growth of the person with whom you are studying.

This may sound unnecessarily obvious. However, we have found that while many people who become chavrusas desire this outcome, what they often end up doing is simply disseminating information and not using the "chavrusaship" as a way to help the student get involved with Jewish life.

We have identified three facets of the chavrusa relationship that, for optimum success with the student, should all be undertaken concurrently.

A. *Teach the student what his heart desires.* Your student should feel that he is gaining something that he wants from the chavrusaship. This may be an understanding of a particular holiday and its customs, how to daven, or an area of Jewish philosophy. Avoid imposing your agenda or priorities on the student. Focus on delivering information in which he expresses interest.

B. *Use your time together to help him grow, not just learn.* Although any Torah learning is certainly going to change the student and help him grow on some level, in order to evoke permanent lifestyle changes you must focus on getting him to see the relevance and truthfulness of Torah Judaism.

Build your chavrusa's understanding that only through Torah will he achieve true fulfillment. Try to show him that Torah is Min ha'Shamayim. Remove any misconceptions that make him think a Torah life will be less satisfying than his current lifestyle.

To the average chavrusa, this may appear to be a daunting task. However, you do not have to accomplish these educational goals all by yourself. Your job is to make sure that they be addressed, either by you or through other means, such as books, tapes, seminars or outreach professionals.

C. *Develop a personal relationship with your chavrusa.* As a friend, in addition to study partner, you will have more impact on his development. Share more than Torah study with him. Share your home, your family and your lifestyle. To really get comfortable with Torah Judaism, the student needs to see and experience Torah living in action. Make an effort to have your chavrusa over for Shabbos or Yom Tov, or invite him for dinner. Create ways to spend time together outside of your study time.

People who take the time to be a chavrusa sometimes feel frustrated in the lack of progress that their student is making. This is usually because they only undertake the first facet of the kiruv process. Only a student who is highly motivated to become frum on his own will progress even if the chavrusa limits his interaction to the first level of kiruv only.

ATTITUDES AND EXPECTATIONS

Although your goal should be to stimulate progress and tangible changes in observance, be careful never to pressure, browbeat or badger your chavrusa into changing. Not only is this wrong, it is highly ineffective.

The mitzvah of tochacha, as explained by Rashi, is to offer *clarification*. This is quite different than the (often abused) translation of "rebuke." Give your chavrusa a chance to learn right from wrong. Do not be overly anxious. If, during your first session, you bombard your chavrusa with 613 mitzvos, thousands of Rabbinical prohibitions and innumerable customs, this is likely to be his last meeting with you.

As your relationship develops, it will often be difficult to decide which areas you should focus on to express your suggestions for change. For this you will need a lot of common sense, even more Siyata D'Sh'maya, and a Rav who has experience with these issues. As a rule, in the early stages of your relationship, it is advisable to ignore your chavrusa's lifestyle and concentrate on teaching him at his own pace.

Chazal teach us "Talmud Torah kneged kol ha'mitzvos kulan, she'hatalmud mayvee liday maaseh." "The study of Torah is greater than all other mitzvos *because study leads to practice.*" Change comes from understanding. When we convey the relevance, beauty, depth and truth of Judaism and correct any damaging misconceptions, the student's level of observance will naturally increase. It will flow and develop genuinely from his newfound clarity.

Torah speaks for itself. We must recognize its power. Our job is to get the message across clearly. If we do, Torah will make the impact.

Sincere Caring

Most importantly, you must truly care about the person you are teaching.

One Sukkos, on a bus in Jerusalem, a religious
man asked a non-religious Jew if he wanted to perform
the mitzvah of shaking the four species. The person
quickly refused.

At the next stop, a second person asked this same
fellow if he would like to shake the four species. The
non-religious Jew donned the other man's yarmulka
and said the proper blessing.

The first man was puzzled by what he saw, so
he inquired as to why his offer was rejected and the
second man's accepted.

The non-religious Jew turned and told him, "There
are two types of Jews. Those who want to *get* mitzvos
and those who want to *give* mitzvos. I sensed that you
wanted to get a mitzvah, while he wanted to give a
mitzvah."

Be certain that in deciding to become a chavrusa, it
is because you want the pleasure of giving, not taking.
If you see your student only as "a mitzvah," he will
quickly sense that and lose interest in learning from
you.

Patience. The Midrash relates us that Rabbi Akiva
once passed by a waterfall at which he frequently
bathed. He noticed an odd-looking rock lying on the
ground. The rock had a hole bored right through its
center. When he looked up, Rabbi Akiva realized that
the rock had been pierced by a continual flow of drops
of water from the waterfall above.

He thought to himself: If water, which is soft, can
bore a hole through a rock, which is hard, all the more

so Torah, which is fire, can make an impression on the heart of man, which is soft.

This realization gave Rabbi Akiva the confidence and motivation to become the great sage he grew to be.[1]

Let us take a lesson from Rabbi Akiva's experience. When he saw the rock, Rabbi Akiva realized that despair has no place in the arena of learning. A drop of water appears to have no impact, yet it is in fact penetrating — so penetrating that it can eventually bore a hole through a rock. All the more potent is the impact of Torah. Although undiscernable, every drop impresses our being, until eventually it causes a breakthrough noticeable to all.

We never know when this breakthrough will happen. But that is not our responsibility. All we have to do is be patient and keep the drops of Torah flowing — and the impact will be made.

EFFECTIVE COMMUNICATION

Have respect for your students. They are intelligent people, who, through their experiences, have gathered much wisdom about life. Just because they do not have a yeshiva education does not mean they will not have very insightful and thoughtful comments or opinions. Chazal teach us in Pirkei Avos, "Who is a wise man? One who learns from every man."

Teach, don't preach. A preacher expects his students to *accept* what he espouses simply on his say-so — not because he has explained to the student why

---

1. Avos D'Reb Nosson, 6:2

his position is truly reasonable. A teacher, on the other hand, shows his students the rationale of his position so they can judge for themselves the merit of what is being said. Unlike the preacher, the teacher wants independent, thinking students.

Be a teacher to your chavrusa, not a preacher. No intelligent, healthy person likes to be preached at.

Be honest. If you are not sure how to answer a question, don't panic. Being a chavrusa does not mean you must know everything there is to know about Judaism. At times you will need to seek outside assistance to answer your student's questions. Do your best to get an answer by the next time you meet, or bring some other resource, whether it is a person, book or tape, to help answer the question. No chavrusaship has ever ended because the student found that his teacher did not know everything.

Create an open atmosphere. It is essential that your discussions take place in a comfortable, non-threatening environment. Create this kind of atmosphere by encouraging your student to ask any question, express any doubt and even voice any criticism. Never allow yourself to feel personally attacked by a question.

Do not be judgmental or condescending. Many people avoid talking to Orthodox Jews because they feel they are being judged or looked down upon. Unfortunately, this perception is sometimes accurate and not merely imagined.

Always remember that you can never judge another person; only God can. The person sitting before you may be a better person and closer to God even though he is unaware of all of the details of observance.

Listen. Listening is a sensitivity which needs to be developed. Wait for cues from your chavrusa before you present your information and ideas, otherwise you may inadvertently present ideas which make him feel unwelcome pressure to make a stronger commitment to Torah. The student must always feel in control and free from pressure to make hasty commitments.

Being an effective listener means more than just paying attention. Tune in to your student's values, his needs, his likes and dislikes. Try to uncover what it is that has distanced him from Judaism as well as what would attract him. Be sensitive to his facial expression and tone of voice. Does it say, "I am interested in what you have to say, tell me more," or, "I need more time to evaluate what you are saying." If you present too much too soon, or step too hard on his perceptions and attitudes, you might turn him off. So tune in, and be aware of how he is responding to what you have to say.

Don't debate. Do not be "quick on the draw" to destroy your chavrusa's ideas or beliefs. If you sense you are offending him, step back and try a softer approach. Our goal is to build bridges, not barricades. If, for example, your chavrusa says that assimilation will curtail anti-semitism, you can disagree with him without ridiculing his opinion.

WHAT TO TEACH

Make it relevant. Chazal advise a person to learn what his heart desires.[2] If your student has very clear-cut

---

2. Avoda Zara 19A

interests then, by all means, study those subjects with him. It is most important that the student feel he is benefitting from the interaction. In learning what he wants to know, the student is more likely to find the experience worthwhile.

On a deeper level, avoid making your teaching academic. Don't treat the Torah as information. Treat it as wisdom, as "Toras Chaim," — instructions for living. Search out what it is that God is trying to teach us to enable us to accomplish our purpose in life. Try to show your chavrusa the wisdom and power of *Jewish living.* As he compares Torah ideas with those of secular society, he will begin to consider incorporating Torah values into his life.

Stay away from giving numerous explanations of the various mefarshim on the meaning of a pasuk. Keep the focus on one point at a time and get right to the core of the matter. Most beginners will not value knowing what the Ramban says on a particularly difficult passage in Chumash, as we do. The students do not know who the Ramban is and cannot appreciate his greatness. The only ideas they will value are those that seem to be immediately beneficial and relevant to their lives.

Following is an example of the "Toras Chaim" approach:

In Parshas Lech Lecha, Hashem says to Abraham, "Lech lecha me'artzecha, u'me'moladetecha, me'bais avicha, el haaretz asher ar'eka." "Go for yourself, from your land, from your birthplace, from your father's house, to the land which I shall show you."

This pasuk appears to be filled with difficulties.

First, if the Torah wanted to tell Abraham to leave his home and go to another land, it would suffice to say "Leave your land, and go to a land that I will show you." Obviously, "birthplace" and "father's house" would be included in that statement. Why the apparent redundancies?

The second problem is the order of the commands. It would seem geographically logical that first you leave your father's house, then you leave your birthplace, then you leave your country.

The third problem is as follows. The Midrash tells us that Abraham was thrown into a fiery furnace by King Nimrod for refusing to serve his idol. Why is the account of "Lech Lecha" considered a greater indication of Abraham's commitment and loyalty to God, to the extent that it was recorded in the Torah while the fiery furnace episode was not? Furthermore, why isn't the test of the fiery furnace considered the first trial? After all, it *preceded* the command for Abraham to leave his homeland. Moreover, isn't giving up your life a much greater challenge than leaving your homeland?

However, the Torah's primary message here is not Abraham's physical departure from his country. Otherwise it would have sufficed to say "Leave your country." This test challenged Abraham to make a different type of departure — a *spiritual* departure — leaving behind the influences, practices and emotional support of society and family — to become truly independent.

The three boundaries (country, birthplace, father's house) represent three different spheres of influence upon each individual, in *ascending* order of intensity. Abraham is commanded to leave his country — to break through the idolatrous influence of his country. He is then commanded to leave his birthplace — to abandon the customs and mores that are reflex to him. Finally, he is challenged to shake loose from the most intense bonds of all: "your father's house" — his primal source of identity and self-esteem.

Surmounting this challenge is Abraham's first step in the development of spiritual independence. Standing alone against the forces of societal and cultural influence, Abraham sets out on the path to become the father of the Jewish nation and earns the title "Avraham Ha'*Ivri*" — Abraham "the Contrarian," who stands firm in his convictions against the entire world.

This was Abraham's primary challenge, and this is the challenge for each one of us. To become an "Ivri," to actualize our potential as Jews, each of us must first sort through the ideas and values that are promulgated to us and decide which are valid and which are false. Then we must develop the intellectual and moral courage to live by what is true, even if the whole world stands opposed. Otherwise we are nothing more than submissive products of our society.

This is the Torah's principal mission for the Jew. And that is why Abraham's first trial is "Lech Lecha" and not the test of the fiery furnace. For in the latter episode, Abraham demonstrated his willingness to give up his life for his beliefs. This is certainly testimony to powerful devotion, but it is a one-time sacrifice. In "Lech Lecha," however, Abraham showed that he was willing to *live* his life according to his beliefs. This is the fundamental test of being a Jew.

Living one's entire life according to an ideal requires a continuous, demanding sacrifice of ego, desire, and habit. To die for a cause is to take pain once; to live for a cause requires ongoing effort. Many are willing to die for the Jewish people, but not all are willing to give up careers, incomes and ways of life to *live* for the Jewish people.

HOW TO TEACH

If at all possible, try to use either Chumash or Pirkei Avos as texts for your chavrusaship. They are among the best sources to convey the practical, relevant wisdom in Judaism. Even if your chavrusa has a particular interest, ask him if it is possible to allot part of your time together to study one of these texts.

Use questions to provoke interest and a desire for answers. A concept which evolves as an answer to a question is usually more appreciated than an idea that you introduce independently. In other words, first create a need for your information. Then proceed to fill it. This will also involve the student in the learning process instead of making him a passive audience.

In preparing a passage to teach, ask yourself the following questions:

a. Are there any obvious redundancies in the passage?
b. Is it grammatically correct?
c. Are there any logical problems?
d. Is there any unnecessary information?
e. Are there any unnecessary words?
f. Are any necessary words missing?
g. Is any necessary information missing?
h. Is this how you would have conveyed the idea?

Before you look to meforshim to answer any difficulties, try to develop your own explanations. Then see if any of your ideas are validated by the commentaries. Using an explanation that you discovered on your own will make your presentation more ardent and forceful, and will make a greater impact on your student.

Gear your presentation to three or four major ideas that can be understood and internalized by the student. Don't overload. Each idea should be accompanied with illustrations that drive your point home.

Your class format should be as follows:

A. Question
B. Answer
C. Illustrate that your answer is true.
D. Draw relevant conclusions and implications for the student's life.
E. Repeat A-D for the next points.

To the best of your ability, put yourself in your student's shoes. What are *his* issues? From what context does *he* view the world? The better you do that, the more you will understand your student and be able to target your information to hit home.

EDUCATE ACCORDING TO HIS WAY

There is a fundamental difference between the teaching of Judaism and the teaching of secular disciplines. When teaching secular subjects, our primary goal is simply to give the student a grasp of the ideas and concepts. When we teach Judaism, however, we have an additional aim of equal importance: We want to motivate the student to internalize the concepts and make them part of his personality.

In explaining how to be an effective educator, Chazal tell us, "Chanoch l'naar al pi darko."[1] To reach

---

1. Mishle 22:6

each student, pay careful attention to his personal inclinations.

In outreach, this principle is crucial. The "student population" is not always ready and eager to learn. Many have built up barriers of resistance to Torah learning and prejudices against a Torah way of life. Each individual must therefore be approached with particular sensitivity to his distinct interests and concerns.

Chazal have given us some keys to facilitate the process of pinpointing and understanding the different natures and motivations of students.

In an essay called "Midos Ha'Avos" in Chelek Beis of Michtav M'Eliyahu, Rav Dessler describes three internal drives that motivate people to action: Chesed, Gevura and Emes.

Rav Dessler explains that each of the Avos embodied one of these characteristics and made it the dominant theme of his Avodas Hashem.

Yaakov's drive was Torah. His primary desire was understanding and comprehension. The 14 years he spent in uninterrupted learning at the Yeshiva of Shem and Aver demonstrates Yaakov's unquenchable thirst for understanding and truth.

In the personality of a secular, twentieth-century Jew, this drive is likely to be manifest in a strong interest in intellectual pursuits, such as philosophy, reading, intellectual discussions, academic or analytical professions. Spare time would probably be spent pursuing hobbies or interests that lead to intellectual development.

Yitzchak's midah was Gevura. His primary motivation was the desire to carry out his responsibilities. His willingness to be a karban to Hashem was symbolic of the dedication of every fibre of his being to a greater cause.

The "gevura" driven people are the doers of the world. A secular Jew does not have a concept of "God's will" as the "right" thing to do. Therefore his energies and abilities are likely to be invested in causes that appeal to him as morally imperative and demanding action. These people also have a tendency to fall into "causes" that society deems necessary or fashionable. Without an objective definition, they look to society as the arbiter of good and bad.

Avraham embodied the trait of Chesed, through which he expressed his primary drive: pleasure. Avraham understood that the greatest possible pleasure is closeness to God, "Ahavas Hashem," and that the best way to attain that pleasure is to emulate God — by giving pleasure to others.

People with Chesed drives are the pleasure seekers. In pursuit of spiritual pleasures, the "Chesed" personality is often drawn to transendental meditation, communing with nature, holistic living, environmental radicalism and mysticism. Without the balanced approach to spirituality that Judaism supplies, these people tend to be less grounded and practical than others. Furthermore, lacking the sophistication to achieve truly sublime pleasures, many of these people misdirect their energies and spend their lives fruitlessly seeking "the experience" in all sorts of temporal, illusory pleasures.

As their offspring and spiritual heirs, each of us is born with a drive similar to either Avraham, Yitzchak or Yaakov. Understanding these drives and how they operate within people will help us teach students "according to their way" and attract them to the personal benefits they will gain from Judaism.

Determining a person's orientation is not a simple thing to do. However, with a little guidance and concentrated effort, it is possible to become adept at this in a relatively short time.

In order to determine the inclination of your student, you must become an active listener. Once you are mentally attuned to this, you will find that people volunteer a lot of clues in everyday conversation about what drives them. The ways they spend their time, conduct their lives and choose their professions are all valuable indicators of specific predilections. Answers to direct questions about what motivated people to make various major choices in their lives (i.e. profession, spouse etc.) will also help identify their primary motivations.

Be Mekarev Him According to His Way

In order to successfully incorporate the advice of our sages, "Educate according to his way," try to be on the lookout for the student's particular drive. Then point out different ways Judaism satisfies that drive.

For the "Torah" personality (drive for understanding), demonstrate the wisdom and depth uniquely available in Torah. Torah is the blueprint of creation and the source of all understanding. To understand the Torah is to understand the world.

For the "gevura" personality, (drive to do "the right thing"), focus on the responsibility to learn about Judaism and to know whether Torah is true in order to determine what obligations one has to himself, his children and his community. You can also point out our responsibility to our ancestors, who sacrificed so much to insure that their children and grandchildren would remain Jewish.

For the "chesed" personality, accentuate the pleasures and beauty of the Jewish lifestyle, the warmth and sense of "belonging" in the community, and the spiritual pleasure and fulfillment available through Torah.

Remember to factor in these drives when you try to interest the student in a particular activity, whether it be inviting him for Shabbos or bringing him to a class. Explain how the activity will be satisfying in terms of *his particular interests*. Keep these drives in mind when you determine what types of programs or people will be particularly interesting and appealing to the student.

Below is a list of books and tapes that are effective at interesting the particular personalities involved.

Spirituality Seekers: The Nine Questions People Ask About Judaism; Strive for Truth; If You Were God; The Way of God; Soul of the Matter; Jewish Meditation; Let Us Make Man; Generation After Generation; The River, the Kettle and the Bird; Waters of Eden; The Jewish Way in Love and Marriage; The Sabbath; Tzitzith — A Thread of Light; Tefillin — God, Man & Tefillin; Teshuva; Choose Life

Responsibility: Anti-Semitism: Why the Jews?; If You Were God; Let Us Make Man; Generation After Generation; The River, the Kettle and the Bird; Doesn't Anyone Blush Anymore?; Made In Heaven; To Be a

Jew; To Pray as a Jew; Book of Our Heritage; Jewish Way in Death and Mourning; Who is a Jew?; Anatomy of a Search; Berel Wein History Tapes; Choose Life

Understanding: Horeb by Rabbi Samson Raphael Hirsch; Anti-Semitism: Why the Jews?; The Nine Questions; Challenge of Sinai; If You Were God; The Way of God; Permission to Believe; The Road Back; Maimonides — The Thirteen Principles of Faith; Jewish Women in Jewish Law; The Sabbath; Who is a Jew?; Challenge — Torah View of Science & Its Problems; Genesis and the Big Bang; Anatomy of a Search; Berel Wein History Tapes; 48 Ways to Wisdom Tapes; Choose Life

Note of Caution: People are sometimes skeptical about using personality identification systems because they seem superficial and open to abuse. Indeed, instead of using a system as a way to broaden one's understanding of people, some readers misinterpret it as a definitive and all-encompassing characterization of a person. Rather than relating to the unique qualities inherent in each individual, they try to fit each person into the textbook caricature.

Obviously this is an improper use of the system and it is certainly not our goal in presenting it. This system is meant only as a beginning. While Chazal tell us that the existence of three distinct traits is a very real phenomenon, we must always take into account the many influences and complexities that shape the interests and characters of the people we are dealing with.

Appendix

DESIGN IN NATURE
AND THE THEORY OF EVOLUTION

What do the wonders of nature tell us about the origin of life? Do they point unmistakeably to the existence of a Designer? Let's look at what our common sense and intuition tell us, what Jewish thought tells us, and finally, what modern science tells us about this question.

In our everyday lives, we can immediately appreciate that the existence of a design means that there was a designer. For example, we ask someone where he obtained a nice sofa we happen to admire, and he replies:

"Oh that? It's an accidental agglomeration of molecules. It simply formed from the dust blowing around the apartment. Over a long period of time, of course."

We know that he is either joking or that he's flipped his lid.

The authors of *The 2001 Principle*,[1] a book on this subject, use a segment from Stanley Kubrick's film, "2001: A Space Odyssey" to demonstrate that our "threshhold" for intuitively recognizing design is reached with an object as simple as a rectangular oblisk.

In the film, the space travelers explore the surface of a newly discovered planet, suspecting that there may

---

1. Gershon Robinson and Ben Yosef (Jerusalem: Hed. Press, 1983)

be some form of intelligent life on the planet. Suddenly, they stumble across a long rectangular metal oblisk. At that instant, the space travelers, along with everyone sitting in the theater munching on their popcorn, stop startled, taken aback. They recognize that someone or something made that bar; some form of intelligent life lives here.

Wherever we turn, we find a natural world of astounding design and complexity. Much of it we simply take for granted. Take your eye, for example. How does this page get transformed into a recognizeable image in your mind? Here are just a few of the specs:

As light enters your eye, about seven million cone-shaped color sensors automatically fine tune your color contrast and detail vision depending on the lighting conditions. Whenever there isn't enough light for an accurate color picture, the cone-shaped sensors sign off and about 127 million rod-shaped, ultra-sensitive black and white sensors switch on. Meanwhile, a computer in your optic nerve receives signals from those 127 million sensors, recodes them and zaps them down a few hundred thousand nerve fibers leading to your brain at about one billion impulses per second. While all this is going on, the pupil is monitoring and maintaining the level of light within your eye, a stereo focusing system is maintaining maximum image sharpness and a sophisticated image-enhancer is clarifying tiny blurs in your vision caused by motion or darkness.[2]

Impressed? You have even fancier equipment. Take your brain. An average human brain has about ten

---

2. Description adapted from *Permission to Believe* by Lawrence Keleman (Jerusalem: Targum, Feldheim 1990) p. 48

billion nerve cells. Each nerve cell sprouts between 10,000 to 100,000 fibers in order to contact other nerve cells in the brain. Taken together, the number of these connections is approximately one thousand million million (that's one quadrillion — mathematicians call it 10 to the 15th power; a 1 followed by 15 zeros.)

Numbers this large are hard to imagine. But let's try. Imagine an area about half the size of the United States (one million square miles) covered by a forest containing 10,000 trees per square mile. If *each* tree contained 100,000 leaves, the total number of leaves in the forest would equal 10 to the 15th power, the number of connections in the human brain!

Despite all these connections, this forest of fibers is not a chaotic, random tangle, but actually a highly organized network where most fibers have specific communication functions and follow regular pathways through the brain. If only 1/100th of the brain's connections were specifically routed, that would still add up to more connections than in the Earth's entire communications network![3]

The dazzling display of intricate design in nature has fascinated man for millenia and modern scientific advances have deepened our understanding of nature's intricacies. Indeed, scientific research in this century alone has uncovered aspects of the universe's structure — from the functioning of human cells to the interplay of the various physical laws which make life on earth possible — which make the previous 2,000 years of design observations pale in comparison.

---

3. Description adapted from *Evolution: A Theory in Crisis*, p. 330, by Michael Denton (London, Burnett Books, 1985)

Most of us have heard of the term "DNA." Deoxyribonucleic acid first became embedded in the popular mind in 1953, when James Watson and Francis Crick were awarded the Nobel Prize for their discovery of the structure and function of DNA, a chain of chemicals found in all living cells. Watson and Crick proved that DNA contains an exact blueprint of the body's every physical detail: fingerprints and toeprints, skin, hair and eye color, heart size and shape. Everything.

In the words of Dr. Michael Denton, an Australian microbiologist:

> . . . The capacity of DNA to store information vastly exceeds that of any other known system; it is so efficient that all the information needed to specify an organism as complex as man weighs less than a few thousand millionths of a gram. The information necessary to specify the design of all the species of organisms which have ever existed on the planet . . . could be held in a teaspoon and there would still be room left for all the information in every book ever written . . . [4]

DNA does this by storing messages in overlapping layers. In theory, for example, a signal code like the Morse code used in military radio transmission can be layered dozens or hundreds of messages deep with a single symbol containing information for two or more words in an overlapping sentence format. (Simplistic example: I a/m/akin/g/oo/d/resses.) In practice, computer scientists have not figured out how to achieve anywhere near DNA's overlap density. Amazingly, DNA stores in a ladder of only a few billion

---

4. *Evolution*, p. 334, Michael Denton

rungs, the designs for body parts made of trillions and trillions of cells.[5]

Scientific research also continues to provide new information showing the unique ability of our earth's environment to support life. Consider:

• Without the presence and precise mixture of carbon, hydrogen, oxygen and nitrogen in our atmosphere, life would not be possible.[6]

• If the earth's average air temperature were to rise by a mere ten degrees, surface rocks would release higher levels of carbon dioxide and stimulate a runaway greenhouse effect, raising temperatures further, evaporating the oceans and destroying all life.

• If the earth's average air temperature would drop by a mere ten degrees, the polar ice caps would increase in size and reflect a higher percentage of solar heat back into space, cooling things down even further. This in turn would cause the glaciers to expand. Within a few years, we would all be frozen solid.[7]

• Had the earth fallen into a slightly closer orbit around the sun, it would have become far too hot to support life.

• Had the earth fallen into a slightly wider orbit around the sun, it would be far too cold to support life.

• If the universe's expansion one second after the Big Bang had been slower by even one part in one hundred thousand million million (that's one in 100 quadrillion, or 10 to the

5. *Permission* pp. 46-48, Keleman

6. *Genesis and the Big Bang*, Chapt. 8, by Gerald Schroeder (New York: Bantam, 1990)

7. *The Anthropic Cosmological Principle*, pp. 567-569, by John D. Barrow and Frank J. Tipler (Oxford, Clarendon Press: 1987)

minus 17th power), the universe would have recollapsed before ever reaching its present size.[8]

There are countless examples from the precisely balanced laws of physics and chemistry which are beyond the scope of this overview.[9]

Jewish Thought

The reasons for our belief in God's existence stem more from the events at Mt. Sinai 3,300 years ago than from philosophical proofs, but in the tradition of "know what to answer a nonbeliever," (Avos, 2:19) the idea of a global design pointing to a Grand Designer has long been part of classical Jewish thought.

The Midrash (Temura, Chapter 3) reports that a nonbeliever once challenged Rabbi Akiva, "Who created the world?"

"The world," Rabbi Akiva replied, "was created by the Lord, Blessed be He."

"Prove it," countered the skeptic.

"Who wove your garment?" asked Rabbi Akiva.

"A weaver, of course," the man answered.

"Prove it," demanded Rabbi Akiva. Rabbi Akiva then turned to his students and said, "Just as the garment testifies to the weaver, the door to the carpenter and the house to the builder, so the does entire world testify to the Holy One, Blessed be He, Who created it."

---

8. *A Brief History of Time*, pp. 121-122, by Stephen Hawking (New York: Bantam Books, 1988)

9. See *Permission* by Keleman, p. 51; Barrow & Tipler, pp. 322-326, 336

Modern Science and the Theory of Evolution

There are two types of explanations for the design we see in our universe: natural and supernatural. Natural explanations fall into two categories: theories that natural forces produce order, and theories that random accidents produced an ordered universe. To date, there is no evidence that natural forces can produce order. In fact, the Second Law of Thermodynamics, known as the Law of Entropy, describes the constant decay of order within the universe.

The Theory of Evolution, however, proposes that, given enough time, random forces can accidentally produce order. This theory is widely assumed by even well educated societies to be a "proven fact." People who question evolution are often viewed with amusement and derided as "creationists" or "fundamentalists." In fact, as we will see, evolution began as a *theory* in need of supporting evidence which never materialized, and has been subject to blistering criticism within the *scientific* community for the past 25 years.

Let's make one thing clear, however. The mere proposition that, *at God's direction*, life arose from dead matter poses no problem for the Torah's worldview. Indeed, it is stated clearly in the Torah, "And God said, 'Let the earth bring forth living creatures after its own kind.'. . ." (Gen. 1:24) The problem with evolution is the proposition that life could arise from inert matter through random, accidental, unguided, unintended events or processes.

Charles Darwin originated the theory of evolution in his now famous 1859 *The Origin of Species*. In the course of his travels and observation of natural life,

Darwin noted that many species of plants and animals developed marked differences in different areas.
Finches (a type of bird) in the Galapagos Islands, for
instance, differed in size, coloring, beak size and shape
from finches in England. Darwin explained these differences as a result of adaptation to their environment.
This phenomenon is known as "micro-evolution" and
it is an undisputed fact. It is what leads tomatoes in
colder climates to grow thicker skins to protect their
inner fruit. It is what requires insecticide producers to
intensify and vary their poison mix as new generations
of insects adapt and bear offspring who are more resistant to the original poison. Finally, it is what requires
pediatricians to vary the types of antibiotic medication
they prescribe for children's middle ear infections because the infection-causing bacteria grow resistant to
the original antibiotics.

Darwin started with the observable fact of micro-
evolution, and hypothesized macro-evolution — that
the various species of plant and animal life which
populate our world evolved from lower, simpler forms
of life. Proposing a process he called "natural selection," Darwin suggested that new species arose when
mutations of existing species would fortuitously turn
out to be stronger or better adapted for survival. Those
individuals possessing the beneficial mutation would
procreate, passing their beneficial mutation on to their
offspring through the gene structure. Hence the term
"survival of the fittest." Darwin proposed that this process was gradual and that new species arose over a
long period of time as a product of a long chain of
small, incremental mutations.

Besides explaining how lower life forms evolved
into more sophisticated ones, Darwin advanced the

hypothesis, later popularized by his neo-Darwinian followers, that life arose from a primordial chemical soup. The reason we do not observe life leaping from inanimate ooze today, Darwin explained, is because any fledgling organisms would now be "instantly devoured or absorbed" by modern ones.[10]

In 1953, a 23-year old University of Chicago graduate student, Stanley Miller, gave this theory a spectacular boost when he recreated what was believed to be the environment of the primeval earth — methane, ammonia, hydrogen and some water. Miller sealed it in a glass apparatus, zapped it with electricity to simulate lightning and within a few days produced a reddish goo rich in amino acids, the building blocks of proteins, the basic stuff of life. Newspaper articles speculated that scientists would shortly conjure up living organisms in their laboratories and demonstrate how life developed in all its complexity.

It didn't work out that way. Miller's amino acids were far from being alive. As we will see, scientists say that the statistical probability of producing simple life forms by chance are exceedingly small. But even if his research had actually produced life, the question would still have remained: Can life arise from random reactions among inorganic molecules? Miller's experiments represent conditions that were not at all random. In his experiments, forces outside the test tube, i.e. the researcher, carefully manipulated the environment within the test tube. As Miller himself, now a professor of chemistry at the University of California at San Diego recently said, "The problem of the

---

10. *Scientific American*, August 1954

origin of life has turned out to be much more difficult than I, and most other people, envisioned."[11]

Similarly, in 1954, a world famous biologist, George Wald, writing in *Scientific American*, presented a seemingly convincing logical argument that random processes following the physical laws of the universe can and indeed did account for the spontaneous generation of life from nonliving matter.

> . . . However improbable we regard this event [creation of life], or any of the steps which it involves, given enough time, it will almost certainly happen at least once . . . Time is, in fact, the hero of the plot. The time with which we have to deal is in the order of two billion years. What we regard as impossible on the basis of human experience is meaningless here. Given so much time, the "impossible" becomes possible, the possible probable, and the probable virtually certain. One has only to wait; time itself performs the miracles. . . .[12]

In 1954, George Wald was a full professor at Harvard and had received the Nobel Prize for his pioneering research into the biochemistry of vision. By presenting his thesis of random events leading to life as proven fact, the general public was left with the mistaken impression that it was indeed fact.

Unfortunately, Wald's skills in mathematical probability and statistics were weaker than his skills in biology.

---

11. Ibid, p. 117
12. *Scientific American*, August 1954

An Unlikely Chance

In 1968, Professor Harold Morowitz, a physicist at Yale University, along with other physicists and mathematicians, expressed concern with the casualness with which certain scientists studying the origins of life were assuming that unlikely events must have occurred. In 1980, *Scientific American* quoted Morowitz in a remarkable article acknowledging that Wald had erred:

> George Wald, in "The Origin of Life," assumes that a primeval soup of organic molecules somehow originated. He then proceeds to show that given enough time, random combinations of molecules might form biologically relevant associations and, ultimately, life. Although stimulating, this article probably represents one of the very few times in his professional life when Wald has been wrong. Examine his main thesis and see. Can we really form a biological cell by waiting for chance combinations of organic compounds? Harold Morowitz, in his book *Energy Flow and Biology*, computed that merely to create a bacterium would require more time than the Universe might ever see if chance combinations of its molecules were the only driving force. As later articles will show, the oldest fossils indicate that the most primitive cells arose early in the history of the Earth. Thus relatively short spans of time were available for the origins of cellular life. . . . During this early era, small organic compounds must accumulate, biological polymers must form, protocells must arise, and a genetic and protein-synthesizing

system must evolve. These events are not consistent with the Wald hypothesis of random associations.[13]

The statistical impossibility of the random creation of life is only the most damning of several problems with the neo-Darwinian theory of evolution. Let's look at some of the other problems with the theory of evolution.

The Fossil Record: It's Not There

In *The Origin of the Species*, Darwin conceded that a gradually evolving series of fossils needed to support his theory had yet to be discovered.

> . . . Geological research, though it has added numerous species to existing and extinct genera, and has made the intervals between some few groups less wide than they otherwise would have been, yet it has done scarcely anything in breaking the distinction between species, by connecting them together by numerous, fine, intermediate varieties; and this not having been affected is probably the gravest and most obvious of all the many objections which may be urged against my views."[14]

While Darwin had faith that paleontologists would one day discover the missing links in the fossil record, more modern research suggests that they will never be found. Professor N. Herbert Nilsson of Lund University,

---

13. *Scientific American*, Special Issue (1980, p. 34) "Life: Origin & Evolution"

14. *The Origin of the Species*, p. 462, Sixth Edition, by Charles Darwin (New York Collier Books, 1962)

Sweden, after 40 years of studying the fossil record, wrote,

> . . . The fossil material is now so complete that the lack of transitional series cannot be explained by the scarcity of the material. The deficiencies are real, they will never be filled . . . [15]

At the 1980 "Conference on Macro-Evolution" in Chicago, the secret was let out to the public that "the fossil record not only does not support the theory — it refutes it." At the conference, the world-famous paleontologist of the American Museum of Natural History, Dr. Niles Eldridge, unequivocally declared, "The pattern that we were told to find for the last one hundred and twenty years does not exist."[16]

In response to the lack of fossil record, together with the statistical impossibility of random mutations gradually spawning new species, Eldridge, together with Harvard paleontologist Stephen Jay Gould, proposed the theory of "punctuated equilibrium," the hypothesis that new species arise not from gradual changes but in sudden bursts of evolution. In this view, species remain largely stable for long periods and then suddenly change dramatically, with all the changes crammed into one or two evolutionary steps. The transition they describe is on the order of a frog giving birth to an alligator or even a chicken. Strange as it may sound, "punctuated equilibrium" allowed these scientists to believe in evolution and explain the lack of fossil record

---

15. Ibid, p. 462

16. *Synthetische Artibildung;* 1954, cited by Francis Hitching, *The Neck of the Giraffe: Where Darwin Went Wrong* (New York: Ticknor and Fields, 1982), p. 22

— since the transition to new species happens so fast, the chance of intermediate forms being fossilized and found is nil.[17]

The proponents of punctuation have never offered an explanation of *how* punctuation accomplishes such dramatic evolutionary changes so rapidly. It is just the only explanation for the appearance of new species, given the gaping holes in the fossil record and the short span of time available for evolution to work. The question still remains, of course, whether punctuation was random, or was directed by some Higher Intelligence. If the proponents of punctuation are proposing that the dramatic changes occurred by chance, they of course will be faced with a much greater statistical improbability than a gradual process. On the other hand, it has been suggested that the account of life appearing in the Torah's Book of Genesis, as understood through the traditional commentaries, closely resembles the theory of punctuation.[18]

Why Don't Snakes Poison Themselves?

Another major difficulty for Darwinian evolutionary theory is the existence of animal organs which cannot be explained as the result of gradual development. Darwin himself wrote in *The Origin of Species*:

> . . . If it could be demonstrated that any complex organ existed which could not possibly have been

---

17. *The New York Times*, November 4, 1980, p. C3

18. *Genesis and the Big Bang*, Dr. Gerald Schroeder, p. 136. The reader is strongly urged to read Schroeder's book. It contains descriptions of several examples where modern science and the Torah's account of Genesis are in harmony.

formed by numerous, successive, slight modifica-
tions, my theory would absolutely break down . . .[19]

Yet, a wide variety of such organs have been identified.
As early as 1917, entomologist Robin John Tillyard,
then professor of zoology at the University of Sydney,
remarked, ". . . The [mating] apparatus of the male
dragonfly is not homologous with any known organ in
the animal kingdom; it is not derived from any pre-
existing organ; and its origin, therefore, is as complete
a mystery as it well could be . . ."[20]

Regarding the origin of carnivorous plants (such
as the Venus Fly Trap) the botanist Francis Ernest
Lloyd in 1942 expressed similar amazement: "How
the highly specialized organs of capture would have
evolved, seems to defy our present knowledge."[21]

Writing in *American Scientist*, Professor Richard B.
Goldshmidt, a biologist with the University of California at Berkeley, challenged his Darwinian colleagues to
explain bird feathers and sixteen other animal organs
that defied evolutionary development, including mammal hair, teeth, mollusk shells, the poison mechanism
of snakes and insect compound eyes.[22]

Snakes' poison mechanisms present a potent challenge to the theory of evolution: the need for *coordinated* evolution of different random mutations. For
example, poisonous snakes have special sacs in which

---

19. *The Origin of the Species*, by Charles Darwin, p. 182
20. *The Biology of Dragonflies*, p. 215, by Tillyard (Cambridge
University Press, 1917)
21. *The Carnivorous Plants*, Lloyd (Waltham: Chronica Botan-
ica Co., 1942)
22. Quoted in Hitching, p. 88

they carry their poison so they don't poison themselves with their own venom. In many species, snakes maintain internal chemical neutralizers to their own poison. Obviously, in the evolution of these snakes, the special sacs and neutralizing agents must have developed (again by random mutation, evolutionists would have us believe), at the exact same time as the poison, otherwise the snakes would not have survived their own poison to procreate and pass on their specially adaptive mutations to their progeny.

The human eye is another example of the need for coordinated evolution. As Francis Hitching puts it, ". . . If the cornea is fuzzy, or the pupil fails to dilate, or the lens becomes opaque, or the focusing goes wrong — then a recognizable image is not formed. The eye either functions as a whole or not at all. So how did it come to evolve by slow, steady, infinitesimally small Darwinian improvements? Is it really possible that thousands upon thousands of lucky chance mutations happened coincidentally so that the lens and the retina, which cannot work without each other, evolved in synchrony? What survival value can there be in an eye that doesn't see? . . ."[23]

Darwin admitted privately to friends moments of doubt over his theory's ability to explain very complicated adaptations or "organs of extreme perfection," as he described them. In a letter to Asa Gray, the American biologist, written in 1861, just two years after the publication of *The Origin of Species*, he acknowledged these doubts and admitted that "the eye, to this day, gives me a cold shudder."[24]

---

23. Hitching, p. 86

24. *Life and Letters of Charles Darwin* (London: 1888) Vol. 2, p. 273, quoted in Denton, p. 326

Another problem: Darwin assumed that any species could slowly evolve into any other species through a series of small changes. But scientists now know that genes can only change a limited amount. This principle was first identified in 1948 by Harvard University geneticist Ernst Mayer. He called it "genetic homeostasis." In hundreds of breeding experiments, geneticists have produced moths of various colors, tomatoes of various sizes, textures and tastes, and fruit flies with bristles ranging from 25 to 56 (the norm is 36) — but they always remained moths, tomatoes and fruit flies.[25] In fact, no new species have been discovered in hundreds of thousands of generations of laboratory fruit flies, nor for that matter, have researchers recorded any new species having evolved in the 120 years since the publication of Darwin's thesis.

Seen Any Nice Mutations Lately?

Another problem: evolution's concept that new species arise as a result of *mutations*. Mutations, of course, usually result in the death or disfigurement of the individual. In fact, no beneficial mutations have been reported since the advent of the theory of evolution. According to Professor Lee Spetner of Bar Ilan University, the probability that even one beneficial mutation would occur in even one individual over the entire course of the most generous estimate of geologic time is so low that it is "unreasonable to assume that it had occurred."[26]

25. See *Permission to Believe*, pp. 57, 58
26. "Natural Selection vs. Gene Uniqueness," *NATURE*, Vol. 226, 1970. p. 948-949

The big problem, of course, is the one we mentioned before — the statistical unlikelihood of random
processes producing anything resembling life.

According to Robert Shapiro, professor of chemistry
at New York University, the odds of a single, viable
bacterium evolving by chance on earth is one in 10 to
the 39,950 power. In arriving at this figure, he allowed
for an amino acid stew covering the surface of the earth
to a depth of six miles and reactions taking place every
second within every cubic *micron* (a sheet of paper is
about 200 microns thick) over a period of one billion
years!

Professor Ernst Chain, a Nobel Prize winning drug
researcher, stated in 1970, "To postulate that the
development and survival of the fittest is entirely a
consequence of chance mutations seems to me a hypothesis based on no evidence and irreconcilable with
the facts."[27]

According to I. Prigogine, a recipient of two Nobel
Prizes in chemistry, "The statistical probability that
organic structures and the most precisely harmonized
reactions that typify living organisms would be gener-
ated by accident is *zero*."[28]

Life From Outer Space

Faced with such statistics, the scientific world is
reevaluating its approach to evolution.

One particularly innovative approach was offered
in 1973, when Dr. Francis Crick, the Cambridge University professor who received the Nobel Prize for DNA

27. Quoted in Hitchings, p. 82
28. *Physics Today*, Vol. 25, p. 23

research, admitted that life could not have evolved by chance on earth and must have been "sent here long ago in the form of germinal material, from elsewhere in the universe."[29]

Crick's solution was attacked by the scientific community as science fiction. Nonetheless, he was joined in 1978 by Sir Fred Hoyle and Dr. Chandan Wickramasinghe, who also abandoned evolution in favor of "the seeding of space by intelligent beings from distant corners of the universe."[30]

Hoyle and Wickramasinghe eventually withdrew their thesis because the odds of obtaining even the enzymes needed for a single protein constituted, "an outrageously small probability that could not be faced even if the whole universe consisted of organic soup."[31]

> No matter how large the environment one considers, life cannot have had a random beginning. Troops of monkeys thundering away at random on typewriters could not produce the works of Shakespeare, for the practical reason that the whole observable universe is not large enough to contain the necessary monkey hordes, the necessary typewriters, and certainly the wastepaper baskets required for the deposition of wrong attempts. The same is true for living material. . . .[32]

If the entire universe couldn't produce a protein by random forces, then it certainly couldn't accidentally

29. Quoted in A.I. Oparih, ed., *Origin of Life*, (Tokyo: Japan Scientific Societies Press, 1978); p. 570

30. *Newsweek*, March 1, 1982, p. 55

31. *Evolution from Space*, Hoyle and Wickramasinghe, p. 24 (London, J.M. Dent & Sons, 1981)

32. Ibid, p. 148

produce any extra-terrestrial, intelligent beings to seed the earth by chance. Where did *they* come from? Hoyle later added for effect that it was more likely that "a tornado sweeping through a junkyard might assemble a Boeing 747 from the materials therein."[33]

Monkey Business

Unfortunately, Stephen Hawking, one of this century's greatest geniuses in theoretical physics, makes a statement in his best-selling science book, *A Brief History of Time*, that appears to downplay all the statistical research on the random origin of life hypothesis.

> It is a bit like the well-known horde of monkeys hammering away on typewriters — most of what they write will be garbage, but very occasionally by pure chance they will type out one of Shakespeare's sonnets. Similarly, in the case of the universe, could it be that we are living in a region that just happens by chance to be smooth and uniform?

In response to Hawking, Dr. Gerald Schroeder, author of *Genesis and the Big Bang*, has calculated the odds of monkeys randomly typing an average Shakespearean Sonnet. He chose the one that opens, "Shall I compare you to a summer's day?"

> There are 488 letters in the sonnet . . . The chance of randomly typing the 488 letters to produce this one sonnet is one in 26 to the 488th power, or one in 10 to the 690th power. The number 10-690 is a

---

33. Shapiro, p. 127

one followed by 690 zeros! The immense scale of this number is hinted at when one considers that since the Big Bang, 15 billion years ago, there have been only 10 to the 18th power number of seconds which have ticked away.

To write by random one of Shakespeare's sonnets would take all the monkeys, plus every other animal on Earth, typing away on typewriters made from all the iron in the universe, over a period of time that exceeds all time since the Big Bang, and still the probability of a sonnet appearing would be vanishingly small. At one random try per second, with even a simple sentence having only 16 letters, it would take 2 million billion years (the universe has existed for about 15 billion years) to exhaust all possible combinations.[34]

Stephen Hawking is a theoretical physicist. In the 1960's, when he was studying the physical-mathematical structure of the early universe, his main collaborator was Roger Penrose. Penrose is a Professor of Mathematics at the University of Oxford and is considered to be one of the top five mathematicians in the world. In a recent book, he discusses the amazing confluence of forces that early universe research indicates was necessary for this life-sustaining universe we live in. Based on the impossibility of the various conditions coming together by chance, Penrose begins to use the word "Creator" and he calculates the odds of all the necessary conditions coming together randomly, at one in $10^{-10^{-123}}$.

How big is that? ". . . Even if we were to write a zero on each separate proton and on each separate neutron

---

34. Please see "Age of the Universe" essay in this volume, by Harold Gans.

in the entire universe — and we could throw in all the other particles as well for good measure — we should fall far short of writing down the figure . . ."[35]

With all the daunting problems facing the theory of random evolution, objective observers have begun to note that the theory's continued, faithful acceptance by scientists has begun to resemble religion more than science. Evolutionists themselves have admitted this.

George Wald, in his famous 1954 *Scientific American* article, wrote:

> One has only to contemplate the magnitude of this task to concede that the spontaneous generation of a living organism is *impossible*. Yet here we are — as a result, I believe, of spontaneous generation.

Professor Harold C. Urey, University of California, Nobel Prize recipient for his work in chemistry:

> All of us who study the origin of life find that the more we look into it, the more we feel it is too complex to have evolved anywhere . . . And yet we all believe as an article of faith that life evolved from dead matter on this planet. It is just that its complexity is so great that it is hard for us to imagine that it did.

Professor A. Weisman, one of the founders of modern genetics, wrote in *The Omnipotence of Natural Selection*:

> Even though I am a believer in the theory of natural selection, I can only say that we have no proof that

---

35. *The Emperor's New Mind*, p. 344, by Roger Penrose (Penguin Books, Oxford University Press)

the initial differentiations and the drastic mutations that took place afterwards in the species have a selective value. However, we are forced to assume this, for otherwise, the entire Darwinian theory of natural selection collapses.

Why do so many scientists feel the need to cling to the theory of evolution despite its tremendous problems? In the history of science, other theories that did not work were discarded. Why is the theory of evolution so important to scientists?

Luckily, we don't have to engage in too much psychological speculation:

> Our faith in the doctrine of evolution depends upon our reluctance to accept the antagonistic doctrine of special creation.
> L.T. More of the University of Cincinnati
> *The Dogma of Evolution*

> Though we may never be able to determine (by means of observation or lab experiment) the process by which a new species was "generated" by means of natural selection in the struggle for survival, we are nevertheless obligated to accept the principle of natural selection because it offers the only explanation of a diversified natural living world, without our having to assume that it was created by a force that desired and created it intentionally.
> Professor August Weisman
> *The Omnipotence of Natural Selection*

Sir Julian Huxley, evolutionist-physiologist, declared in Chicago that he was an atheist and that Darwin's real achievement was to remove the whole idea of God as the creator of organisms from the sphere of rational discussion.

N. Macbeth, *Darwin Retried*

The reluctance to reject evolution springs from a profound antagonism to the only alternative — God. Why do so many scientists refuse to face the music? Let's try to explain. While admitting that we're speculating, there are certain generalizatzations we can make.

For modern man, sciences define reality. Ice cream flavors and clothing choices are a matter of taste; politics is a matter of opinion. But chemistry, physics, biology, paleontology — they're real, they're truth.

There are good historical reasons why we moderns have adopted this world view.

The Enlightenment awakened in Western civilization a reverence for man's power of reason and our ability to understand and control our world. Advances in scientific understanding led to the Industrial Revolution. This revolution has led, step by step, to our present level of technology. Man on the moon, laptop computers, program trading, medicine, hydrogen bombs, microwave ovens, washers, dryers, cars, trains, airplanes, central heating, electricity, telephones, television, microchips, et al —are all the products of scientific inquiry and its applied technology.

The process by which science arrives at its conclusions is objective and testable. The products of its technology are real, tangible and have profoundly improved the physical quality of our lives. Science has also given us the very satisfying feeling of being able to understand and control our physical world. The history of man prior to the Enlightenment was a history of being mystified by and at the mercy of an incomprehensible nature. It doesn't matter much that the TV weatherman is wrong as often as he is right. It feels good to *think* that he knows what he's talking about.

The modern perception of an unbridgeable gap between science and religion needs to be understood in the same historical context. At the same time that Enlightenment philosophies and scientists were expanding the bounds of human reason, the Catholic Church stood firmly opposed to the results of any inquiry that challenged its narrow conception of Biblical revelation. (Galileo's discovery that the earth revolved around the sun was only the most famous display of this opposition.)

The intellectual history of Western civilization was thus written; that religion was "faith" and stood opposed to rational inquiry. Judaism got thrown in by association.

Nothing could be further from the truth. Science and revelation are two different ways of discovering truth. We just need to be sure we're evaluating scientific and revelation claims objectively. Recent research has revealed an amazing confluence between scientific research and our Torah's description of the world. (See Gerald Schroeder's *Genesis and the Big Bang: The Discovery of Harmony Between Modern Science and the Bible*.)

The Torah tells us that resistance to facing reality stems from *gaava* and *taava*, arrogance and physical desire. "Do not chase after your heart and your eyes which lead you astray." (Numbers 15:38)

A. Huxley's "Confession of a Professed Atheist" (Report, June 1966) provides an amazingly honest example of how one's desires cause him to see the world the way he *feels* like seeing it:

> I had motives for not wanting the world to have meaning; consequently assumed that it had none, and was able without any difficulty to find satisfying reasons for this assumption . . . For myself, as no doubt, for most of my contemporaries, the philosophy of meaninglessness was essentially an *instrument* of liberation. The liberation we desired was simultaneously liberation from a certain political and economic system and liberation from a certain system of morality. We objected to the morality because it interfered with our sexual freedom.

The kind of cognitive dissonance that is caused by arrogance, can be seen in scientists' desire to be able to explain and control a world without reference to anything but ourselves. Robert Jastrow was a self-professed "atheist" who changed his self-description to "agnostic" (not sure) when he realized the eerie similarity between contemporary astrophysical research (the Big Bang) and the Bible's account of creation.

> . . . scientists cannot bear the thought of a natural phenomenon which cannot be explained, even with unlimited time and money. There is a kind of religion in science; it is the religion of a person who believes there is order and harmony in the Universe, and every event can be explained in a rational way as the product of some previous event; every effect must have its cause; there is no First Cause . . . This religious faith of the scientist is violated by the discovery

that the world had a beginning under conditions in which the known laws of physics are not valid, and as a product of forces or circumstances we cannot discover. When that happens, the scientist has lost control. If he really examined the implications, he would be traumatized. As usual, when faced with trauma, the mind reacts by ignoring the implications — in science this is known as "refusing to speculate" — or trivializing the origin of the world by calling it the Big Bang, as if the Universe were a firecracker.

Now we would like to pursue that inquiry farther back in time, but the barrier to further progress seems insurmountable . . . For the scientist who has lived by his faith in the power of reason, the story ends like a bad dream. He has scaled the mountains of ignorance; he is about to conquer the highest peak; as he pulls himself over the final rock, he is greeted by a band of theologians who have been sitting there for centuries.

Robert Jastrow
God and the Astronomers, p. 112-116

A TIME FOR ACTION

The following essay is based on a call to action issued by Hagaon Horav Moshe Feinstein, Shlita, to yeshiva students, in view of the extraor-dinary nature of our times. We believe that it has broad implications to every individual's responsibility to act on behalf of his fellow Jew.

The Priority

"FIRST CORRECT YOURSELF, AND THEN CORRECT OTHERS" (*Sanhedrin* 18a). It is indeed a great *mitzvah* to bring others close to Torah. First, however, one must strengthen his own commitment to Torah.

Yeshiva years are a time when one must concentrate on self-improvement. During one's youth, one must make Torah study his full time occupation, striving for greatness in Torah. A student must use every emotion to bring himself close to Torah. Even traits generally considered negative, such as envy, must be harnessed to further one's growth in Torah, as the *Gemora* advises: "*Envy among scribes increases wisdom*" (*Baba Basra* 21a). Like King David, his cry must be "*My soul thirsts for You*" (*Tehillim* 63:2). This must supersede all other involvements. Only after one has developed his own powers in Torah can one assume responsibility for others.

This sequence is reflected in our prayers, when we ask G-d to give us the power "*to learn and to teach.*" First we must learn, then we can teach others.

Today, however, a crisis situation exists, and it is most acute. While there were times when we could keep ourselves distant from forces of darkness, they are now closing in, even threatening the most sheltered communities of those loyal to Torah. In addition, many people estranged from Torah are searching for the truth of Torah: These are exceptional times. We must therefore examine our accepted priorities to determine who is to be charged with the responsibility of battling to better our situation and under what conditions.

Prerequisites: Accepting Authority of the Torah Leadership

THE FIRST STEP IN THIS EXAMINATION is the establishment of guidelines. Rules must be strictly adhered to, even when bringing people close to Torah, and unless one follows them, he can do more damage than good.

The most basic of rules is to follow the directives of our Torah leadership, especially in the area of *kiruv rechokim* (reaching out to those estranged from *Yiddishkeit*), where there is always a temptation and rationalization to compromise and to make concessions. While every discipline has its experts, and people generally recognize that one can only succeed if he follows their advice, in *kiruv rechokim* there are too many self-styled experts, who believe that they know more than *Gedolei Torah*. Too often, their ideas can accomplish more harm than good. Worse yet, they consider such matters outside the expertise of our Torah leaders and feel that they are not obligated to follow their teachings, even making light of their advice. This approach, in itself, is as great an evil as that which they are setting out to overcome, for it does violence to a central aspect of the Jewish commitment: the authority vested in the Torah leadership of each generation, as an integral part of *Torah sheba'al Peh* (the Oral Law).

1973

The *Gemora* tells of a heathen who came to Hillel to be converted to Judaism (*Shabbos* 31a). The heathen was willing to accept both the Written Torah and the Oral Law—as Rashi explains—but he refused to recognize the interpretations of Shammai and Hillel as part of the Oral Law spoken by G-d. Nonetheless Hillel accepted him. Hillel was confident (Rashi continues) that once he taught the heathen, the latter would come to depend upon him. Rashi's explanation of this incident illustrates that belief in the Oral Law is totally dependent upon the acceptance of the teachings of the *Gedolei Hador*.

This authority must be granted to the leaders of each generation, regardless of their relative merit to leaders of other generations—"*Yiftach in his generation is like Shmuel in his*" (*Rosh Hashana* 25b). Even though the prophet Shmuel was undoubtedly greater than Yiftach, the latter still merited ultimate respect as the Torah leader of his own generation. Greater sages have existed in earlier times, but our obligation is to follow those of our age.

One who does not accept the Torah leaders of his generation cannot claim to believe in the Oral Law. Thus a person who does not subjugate himself to our Torah leaders, even though he may be religious in every other respect, is not qualified to lead others in kiruv rechokim.

Who Can Lead the Searchers? WHEN PRESENTED WITH THE OPPORTUNITY to engage in endeavors outside of his personal growth, the *ben Torah* will normally defer to others. He assumes that there are others who are equally qualified to handle the problem at hand, if not more so. Now that so many irreligious people are seeking truth, we might hope that there are enough interested parties who are qualified to meet their needs. Unfortunately, this is not so, for the very ones who claim to offer them truth are often further from it than the seekers, and might even be described as being ensnared in an idolatry of sorts:

The Torah warns "*Do not turn to the idols*" (*Vayikra* 19:4), which the *Gemora* explains as a reference to conceptual idols, ideologies not based on the Torah (*Shabbos* 149a). Unless one follows the Torah meticulously, he can even make idols of his own ideas. This unstructured and uninhibited "freedom of thought" is frequently the hallmark of many who are engaged in enlightening those who are seeking, and unquestionably disqualifies them from the task.

Yet those who seek guidance must be led by someone. He who leads others must be extremely firm in his faith. He must not follow his own whims, but must base his entire ideology on G-d's Torah. He must be meticulous in adhering to the teachings of our Torah leaders, and must not be misled by false ideologies or foreign methodologies. *This leaves us none but the ben Torah, whose spiritual stamina is fortified by the Torah as taught by the heads of our great yeshivos. Only he is equipped to address the masses and return them to the truth.*

The Reluctant Redeemer BUT THE YESHIVA STUDENT MAY INSIST that he can offer the world much more by devoting himself fully to his Torah studies, his primary obligation. One is not permitted to interrupt Torah study for any *mitzvah*, unless it is a personal obligation (such as *tefillin* or reciting *Shma*). Indeed, our People's greatest teacher and prime redeemer, Moshe Rabbeinu, actually would have preferred to abstain from leading the Jewish People from bondage to freedom. He realized that he could accomplish much more through his personal involvement in Torah.

The Midrash tells of Moshe's unwillingness to assume leadership in four major assignments: pleading to Pharaoh for the release of *Bnai Yisroel*, splitting the *Yam Suf*, ascending Mount Sinai to receive the Torah, and entering the newly erected *Ohel Mo'ed* (the tabernacle). In each of these cases Moshe stood aside until G-d commanded him to lead: "*You must, for there is no one else!*"

66

1973

Thus, the yeshiva student's predilection to abstain has a precedent. But by the same token so does the necessity that he become actively involved, in exceptional circumstances. As Moshe responded to the voice of authority when it told him that he must because there was no one else, so too must our yeshiva students. As mentioned before, there are no others who are qualified for the task. Under such circumstances, Torah study must also be interrupted.

Another factor that enlarges the obligation on those who are capable of bringing others closer to Torah is the fact that many people who are far from a Torah life can be categorized as a *Tinokos Shenishbu,* people held captive by Gentiles since infancy (*Yoreh De'ah* 159:6). It is a *mitzvah*—an obligation—to bring such individuals back to the Torah and Judaism (*Mishneh Torah, Hilchos Mamrim* 3:3). When there is no one else to accomplish this, then one must even take time from his Torah studies to do so.

In summary. one must emulate Moshe. who was a leader because he had no choice.

The "Teach or Learn" Dilemma

THERE IS ALWAYS THE DEFENSE against active involvement in teaching others: *Must I sacrifice my own growth?*

The *Gemora* teaches us: "A man and his son must both study Torah. When possibilities exist for only one, a man's personal needs take precedence to his son's" (*Kidushin* 29b, *Yoreh Deah* 245:2). One may not even take time from his own Torah studies to teach his son, unless he knows that his son's potential is greater than his own. This is a highly significant point: If one's own studies take precedence over teaching his own child, then they certainly take precedence over teaching strangers.

Yet we find that Rabbi Preda had a student with whom he reviewed each lesson 400 times. As a reward for this, 400 extra years were allotted to his life, and everyone in his generation was guaranteed a place in the World to Come (*Eruvin* 54b).

One would assume that Rabbi Preda could have gained more knowledge had he used this time for his own study. To be sure, when one teaches, he also learns, in keeping with Rabbi Chanina's statement: "I have learned much from my teachers, more from my companions, and most of all from my students" (*Taanis* 7a). Rav Chanina's maxim, however, obviously did not apply to a student such as Rabbi Preda's. In addition, no one can grow exclusively from teaching; each individual must also study for himself.

What is apparent from this is that even though an individual's own studies take precedence over another's, he must still find time to teach others.

In Search of a Time-Formula

A MAJOR QUESTION REMAINS, HOWEVER: *How much time can and must one devote to this task?*

A rule of proportions for giving of personal resources to others can be inferred from the laws of charity. (We find a similar parallel in *Tana DeBei Eliahu Rabbah* 27.) A person must have enough to take care of his own personal needs before he gives charity (*Tur Yoreh De'ah* 151). Nevertheless, this is not to be taken so literally as to totally exempt a person who does not have everything he needs from giving charity (*Yoreh De'ah* 248:1). There is always some measure that one must do for others.

The same is true of our own Torah needs. Beyond question, one's primary obligation is to his own studies. One can never say that he has amassed enough to meet his personal needs, for Torah "is longer than the earth and broader than the sea." One must therefore give his own studies precedence, but this must not be absolute. One must also act on behalf of others.

67

1973

As in charity, where one has an obligation to give a tenth of his income to the poor, so must one spend one tenth of his time working on behalf of others, bringing them close to Torah. If one is endowed with greater resources, he must correspondingly spend more of his time with others.

The Pitfalls of Our Times

ONE CANNOT CONTEMPLATE INVOLVEMENT with fellow Jews in more worldly circumstances, even for the higher purpose of winning them to a Torah commitment, without taking note of the risks and pitfalls that abound today. It is in place to issue words of caution as well as words of encouragement in this regard.

Today's situation has special pitfalls peculiar to our times. Many people feel that they can partake of the worldly along with Torah. They do not realize that this world is the portion of Eisav, and not of Yaacov (*Devarim Rabbah* 1:17). They want to indulge in all worldly delights, in a kosher manner; should a commodity or activity carry a kosher label, they even consider it a *mitzvah* to pursue it. This brings people to lose valuable time from their Torah studies, and in some respects the situation has reached tragic proportions. Most certainly, then, if one hopes to bring others to Torah, he must make Torah the primary focus of his life. It is thus incumbent upon us to divorce ourselves from worldly pursuits to the greatest extent possible. Our sages went so far as to contemplate completely destroying all evil urges *(yetzer hora)*. They did not fully execute this plan because a measure of *yetzer hora* is essential for the continuance of the course of nature. Nonetheless, they sought to reduce pursuit of worldly desires to the greatest degree possible.

When faced with this warning to avoid entanglements in worldly pleasures and distractions, one might well be reluctant to engage in any pursuit other than Torah study—even for the ultimate purpose of bettering the lot of others through *kiruv rechokim.* But the current situation makes urgent demands upon us, for *"It is a time to work for G-d, they have abandoned Your Torah"* (*Tehillim* 119:126). Indeed, one must devote the major portion of his time to Torah study, but there are times when we must set Torah study aside and implement Torah action for G-d's sake, to bring the truth to others.

When one does this in the manner prescribed by our Torah leadership, then G-d will give him strength so that association with people estranged from our religion will not harm him.

When one follows the ways of Torah, he is indeed protected by G-d from all harm. It is in this spirit that the Torah tells us: "Yaacov came complete to the city of Shechem" (*Bereishis* 33:18). Rashi comments that he returned from Lavan complete in body, possessions, and Torah. He had followed the way of the Torah, and no harm could befall him. □

NOVEMBER 1973

1973

FROM THE WRITINGS OF THE CHOFETZ CHAIM ON THE OBLIGATION OF KIRUV

לג.

מאמר „עת לעשות לד'".

הנה ידוע לכל שעיקר בריאת העולם היה בשביל התורה
כדכתיב „אם לא בריתי יומם ולילה, חוקות שמים וארץ לא
שמתי', והנה ראה ראינו. כי התורה מתמוטטת מיום אל יום
ומועטים המה הלומדים הנמצאים בישיבות הגדולות ואלו הנמצאים

---

*) וידעתי גם ידעתי, שימצאו אנשים משימתם אשר ילעגו לזה, ולא ארכש
לי כבוד מהם. אבל כבר אמרו אשרי המותר כבודו מפני כבוד המקום

עז

החפץ חיים

ערך התורה וגדלותה ללחום מלחמת התורה, בכל מקומות
מושבותיהם בכל האמצעים, עי"ז שילמדו בעצמם וע"י שייסדו
חבורות בעיירותיהם ללמוד התורה, וכמו שמצינו ביהושפט, כאשר
לקחו ממנו איזה עיירות צעקו אל ד' להשיב להם, ואף כי יכלו
להתקיים מבלעדי הערים הללו, ומה גם כשהיצר וכת דילי'
מתגברים לגזול ממנו את תורתנו, אשר היא נשמת חיינו ואשר
מבלעדה אין חיינו חיים, אעכו"כ צריכים אנחנו ללחום בכל
כוחותינו עבור קיום תורה"ק, על בעלי תורה הללו להשתדל
לאהב ש"ס על כל אחינו ב"י, איש איש בעירו בכל המדינות,
שיכבדו את התורה הקדושה ויסלסלוה וירוממוה, ועי"ז יתרבה
כבוד ד' בכל העולם, ומלחמה כזאת היא לא מלחמת רשות, כי
אם מלחמת מצוה, שהכל חייבים לקחת חלק בה להגן על כבוד
ה' ותורתו, ואיש את רעהו יחזק לשמור תורתנו הקדושה שלא
תרד ירידה כללית ח"ו, ואז בודאי יעזרנו השי"ת למען שמו
הגדול, אמן.

אדר, תרפ"ו.

הולכים ומתמעטים משנה לשנה, וחלילה תשתכח תורה מישראל.

והנה בשנים שמלפנינו שכל ישראל היו מכניסים בניהם לביה״ט כשר ותלמוד תורה, היינו יכולים לקוות שהבנים הקטנים יתגדלו ונכנס מהם לישיבות, אבל כעת שנכנסים לביה״ס כשר רק מעוטא דמעוטא ורובא דרובא נכנסים לביה״ס החילוניים אשר לבד שאין בהם לימוד תורה דת ואמונה, כל מגמתם להתנגד לדת קדשינו, את תוה״ק קרעוה לגזרים ועשו ממנה ספורים בלי שום אמונת אמן.

ואותו המועט הנכנס לחדר כשר, הוא לכל היותר רק עד בני אחת עשרה או שתים עשרה שנים, ומאין יתגדלו בעלי גמרא (ומי יאמר, אלו שצריכים לצאת להוראה?) אוי ואבוי לנו, שכל המון בית ישראל, אפילו הכשרים שבכשרים, ישארו אנשים פשוטים, ואפסו בעלי תורה, וכל זה יהי׳ רק בעשר שנים הראשונות, ואם ח״ו ימשך עוד איזה שנים במצב כזה, יהיו הכל בורים ממש, שלא ידעו אפילו פסוק חומש, ומאין יהי׳ קיום התורה בכללה, אפילו בדברים שהם חמורים מאד שצריכים ליהרג ולא לעבור עליהם כאיסור עריות ונדה בכללה, וקדושת שבת שהיא יסוד התורה, וכן איסור דם וחלב שיש על זה כרת וכן שאר מאכלות אסורות, כמו בשר טרפה ונבלה ובשר בחלב ובשר חזיר וכה״ג. כלל הדבר, אין לערוך ואין לשער גודל הריסות התורה, ובהמשך הזמן יהי׳ נכשלים ח״ו באיסור התחתנות ישראלים עם נכרים, וכבר נטל השטן חלק גדול מאתנו בהרבה מקומות בחוץ למדינתנו.

והנה בעניני העולם מצינו, שכל אחד ואחד מתושבי מדינתו מחויב לעבוד בצבא שנתים או שלש שנים ואח״כ חוזר לביתו ולעבוד לעבודת עצמו, ואם אירע לפעמים שנשמע שמדינה אחת מתכוננת לערוך מלחמה נגד מדינתם מתאספים שרי המלוכה והמדינה, להתבונן בתכסיסי המלחמה, אם יש בכחם להלחם עם אויביהם, וכשרואים שחיילים מועטים וגם מזון כדי צורך החיל המועט אין להם, מוציאים פקודה: א) שכל אנשי המדינה מחויבים להתלמד תכסיסי מלחמה ולמשוך בקשת אפילו האציל

שבאצילים על משך זמן קצר, כדי שיהיו כולם מוכנים למלחמה
לעת הצורך. ב) מחויבים כל אנשי המדינה להפריש כל אחד
איזה סכום מכספו שיהי׳ די ספוק לצרכי החיל והמלחמה על
משך שנה ושנתים לכה״מ.

כן הדבר בעניננו, חלול השם גדול בכל עבר ופנה
והקב״ה מתאונן, ע״ז מאד וכדכתיב ביחזקאל. ומה שלפנים היתה
הירידה בדת במשך עשר שנים יורד כהיום באיזה חדשים והתורה
מתמוטטת מיום ליום, והיצה״ר עורך מרידה גדולה ונוראה נגד
מלכנו ממ״ה הקב״ה, החובה לענ״ד על כל הרבנים וגדולי
ישראל וכן על הלומדים שבכל עיר ועיר להתאסף יחד ולטכס
עצה, במה נחזיק מעמד נגד היצה״ר ואיך ובאיזה אופן לערוך
אתו מלחמה כדי לקדש כבוד השי״ת ולהציל תוה״ק מירידה
כללית ח״ו.

וכשם שבעניני העולם בזמן המלחמה מחויב כל אחד
מאזרחי המדינה לצאת למערכות המלחמה נגד האויב, וכל אחד
יאמר לחברו הבא ונתחזק בעד עמנו וארצנו, לא עת לנו לשבת
בחיבוק ידים ואין לנו לחכות עד שיבוא האויב בגבולינו, אלא
עלינו לאזור מקודם שארית כוחותינו, וכל מי שיודע תכסיסי
מלחמה מחויב ללמוד את מי שאינו יודע, ואפילו האציל
שבאצילים, אף שפטור בזמן שיש שלום בארץ מכל צרכי המלחמה
מ״מ בזמן מלחמה הנוגע לקיום המדינה, גם הוא מחויב לעמוד
על המשמר וגם הוא צריך לצאת למלחמה נגד האויב. כן הדבר
בעניננו בימינו אלה, שהמרידה נגד הקב״ה ותורתו הולכרת
ומתרבה מיום ליום, ואם נשב כעת בחבוק ידים כל עוד שלא
נתגברה כ״כ המרידה, ולא נקדם פני הרעה מי יודע מה יולד
יום ואם לא נאחר ח״ו הזמן אף שאח״כ כבר נרצה לתקן אולי
לא יהי׳ בידינו ח״ו.

ע״כ על כל אחד ואחד שיש רק מעט אור תורה בתוכו
כל אחד לפי מה שהוא, ישתדל לעשות בזה כפי כוחו, אם יודע
מקרא, יעשה חבורה וילמד לאחרים מקרא, אם יודע משנה יעשה
חבורה לומדי משניות וילמד עמהם, וכן אם יודע ללמוד דף
גמרא, החוב עליו לעשות חברה ולקבוע עתים ללמוד לפניהם

דף גמרא בכל יום, ואל יאמר האציל והוא הת"ח שלמד
מלפנים כמה שנים בישיבה, ויש לו ידיעה רבה בתורה, שהוא
פטור מזה, אלא גם הוא מחויב לצאת למערכי המלחמה ועליו
ליסד חבורות ללמוד תורה כפי יכלתו, ולא עוד אלא הוא מחויב
יותר מאיש אחר ועליו לזרז ולעודד ולהקהיל קהלות ברבים,
ולהוכיחם ולהורותם דרך הישרה, והעיקר שעל בני תורה שבכל
עיר ועיר לפקוח ולהשג.ח על למוד תנוקות של בית רבן ולהשתדל
בכל יכלתם, שיהיו בתי הת"ת מתכוננים על טהרת הקודש עם
למוד גמרא ולבחון את תלמירי החדרים והת"ת מפרק לפרק.

ויש עוד עצה כללית ע"י לומדי התורה שהם יוכלו להציל
את התורה מירידה כללית והיינו: שכל אחד שלמד מלפנים
באיזה ישיבה, הן באלו עשר שנים והן מלפנים, ינדב את עצמו
כעת לכבוד ד' ותורתו שלא תשתכח ח"ו, לקבוע עתים ללמוד
איזה שעות ביום, יש שינדב ג' שעות, ויש שתי שעות, ואלו
השעורים גופא יש שיסכים לנהוג כן בקביעות ג' שנים ויש שתי
שנים ולכל הפחות שנה אחת. (ולא שיסע מביתו לאיזה מקום
תורה אלא בעירו גופא יקבע מקום וזמן ללמוד בכל יום) ונכון
מ.אד לכתחלה ליסד חבורה לזה אשר בשם „זכרו תורת משה"
תכונה, שעי"ז יתקיים הדבר ביותר ויתגדל שם שמים עי"ז וכמו
שאחז"ל באבות: עשרה שיושבין ועוסקין בתורה שכינה שרויה
ביניהם, ואפילו אם לא תהי' חבורה של עשרה כ"א פחות מזה
ג"כ טוב יותר ללמוד בחבורה מלמוד ביחידות כמבואר שם.
(ומי שהוא טרוד בעסקיו וצריך לנסוע לרגלי מסחרו שבוע או
שנים אזי יעשה חשבון בעצמו כמה שעות בטל במשך זמן נסיעתי
ולכשישוב לביתו בהצלחה צריך לידע, שיש עליו חוב שצריך
לפורעו, דוגמא מה שאחז"ל בגמרא על רב אחא בר יעקב
„דיזיף ביממא יפרע בליליא", וראוי שיתבוננו בני תורה תלמידי
הישיבות להתאסף יחד מזמן לזמן להתבונן בחזוק התורה ולחשוב
מחשבות בעצה מה לעשות להגדיל למוד התורה.

ובאמת כאשר נתבונן על מצב התורה, אשר ירדה פלאים
בעו"ה בשנים האחרונית, אז יגדל החוב על כל בעלי תורה
שלמדו מלפנים בהישיבות או בקבוצים, היודעים ומבינים את

הנמצאים בכל עיר ועיר

קול נשמות אחיך קוראים לך

בס"ד

אנו עדים לתופעה מעודדת ומעוררת תקוה, למראה רבים מאחינו החוזרים בתשובה, ומשליכים מאחורי גוום משרות מכובדות, וקובעים עצמם לשקוד על דלתי התורה בישיבות, בפגישות המתקיימות עם אחים תועים, תינוקות שנשבו שחונכו על ברכי החינוך הכפרני, נשמעים הרהורי תשובה, ובפיהם משאלה ללמוד את יסודות היהדות ולהתקרב לחיי תורה.

יהודים אלו נמצאים בשכונותנו, בכל עיר ועיר, ובכל מקום, מכל עדה ומכל חוג, ובכוחנו להעיר את רוחם, במיוחד בימי הרחמים והרצון כשלב כל יהודי מתעורר להתקרב אל ה'.

אוי לנו מיום הדין
אוי לנו מיום התוכחה!

אם בעת כזאת נעמוד מנגד, ולא נצא אל אחינו לעוררם לחזור בתשובה, וכשיבואו המקטרגים ויתבעו החוטאים לדין על עוונותיהם, יעוררו החוטאים הדין על ראשי העדה ויראי ח' הנמצאים בכל עיר, דכל מי שיש בידו למחות באנשי עירו ואינו מוחה נתפס על אנשי עירו, כמבואר במסכת שבת (נ"ד ע"א) גבי פרתו של רבי אלעזר בן עזריה, וע"ז רמז הנביא יחזקאל (ל"ד, ד') "את הנחלות לא חזקתם ואת הנדחת לא השבתם ואת האובדת לא בקשתם וגו' ודרשתי את צאני מידם."

ולפעמים נתפס האדם גם בעודו בחיים בזה העולם על שנמנע ממצוע תוכחה, כמובא במס' שבת (נ"ה ע"א) א"ר אחא ב"ר חנינא : מעולם לא יצאה מדה טובה מפי הקב"ה וחזר בה לרעה, חוץ מדבר זה דבתחילה אמר הקב"ה לגבריאל לך רשום על מצחן של צדיקים תיו של דיו, שלא ישלטו בהם מלאכי חבלה, (בעת חורבן ירושלם) ואחרי שקטרגה מדת הדין ואמרה "רבש"ע היה להם למחות ולא מיחו" ואף שהיה גלוי וידוע לפני הקב"ה שאם היו מוחין לא היו מקבלים מהם, נתהפך גזר דינם לרעה, וגזר עליהם ממקדשי תחלו, תני רב יוסף אל תקרי ממקדשי אלא ממקדשי ; אלו בני אדם שקיימו את התורה כולה מאלף עד תיו.

ומובא ברמב"ן בשם חירושלמי בסוטה אקרא "ארור אשר לא יקים את דברי התורה הזאת לעשות אותם" אמר רבי אסי בשם רבי תנחום בר חייא : למד ולימד שמר ועשה והיח סיפק בידו לחחזיק ולא החזיק, הרי זה בכלל ארור. ידרשו בהקמת חזאת, בית המלך והנשיאות שבידם לחקים את התורה ביד חמבטלים אותה, ואפילו היה הוא צדיק גמור במעשיו, והיה יכול לחחזיק התורה ביד הרשעים המבטלים אותה, הרי זה בכלל ארור.

אי לזאת, חוב גדול על כל הצבור שומרי תורה ומצוות, אשר כבוד שמים נוגע ללבו לחזק בדקי היהדות ובמיוחד ללמד תועים בינה, ולקרב רחוקים לחיק היהדות, יארגנו כל קהילות ישראל בראשות הרבנים להקדיש כל אחד לפחות ערב אחד בימים אלו, לצאת באזור הקרוב, ולבקר מספר משפחות שהתרחקו מחיי תורה, ולשוחח עמם בידידות מתוך אהבה ולהסביר להם יסודות האמונה ועיקרי המצוות כל אחד כפי הבנתו, ולעוררם לחזור בתשובה.

וד' יהיה בעזרנו להקים עולה של תורה ויחתמנו לחיים טובים ולשנת גאולה וישועה.

אליעזר מנחם מן שך   יעקב ישראל קניבסקי   חיים שמואלביץ

GLOSSARY OF HEBREW TERMS AND PHRASES

"AIN TZADDIK BA'ARETZ ASHER YAASEH TOV V'LO YECHETA": "There is no one on earth who only does good and never makes mistakes"

APIKORES: heretic

AREIVUS: inter-responsibility among Jews

"ASHREINU MAH TOV CHELKEINU, U'MAH NAIM GORALEINU": "How fortunate are we that our portion is so good and that our lot is so pleasant"

AVAIROS: mistakes

BARUCH HASHEM: Thank God

"CHANOCH L'NAAR AL PI DARKO": "Educate a child according to his way"

CHAZAL: acronym for "our rabbis, of blessed memory"

CHESED: lovingkindness

CHOFETZ CHAIM: Rabbi Yisrael Meir HaCohen

CHUMASH: The Five Books of Moses

DERECH ERETZ: character refinement

DVEYKUS B'HASHEM: attachment to God

EMES: truth

FRUM: Yiddish for "observant"

GEVURA: strength

"HOCHAYACH TOCHIYACH": "You shall surely rebuke"

ISH: man

ISHA: woman

KARBAN: sacrifice
KEDUSHA: sanctity
"KIBUD AV V'AIM": commandment to honor one's fa-
    ther and mother
KIDDUSH HASHEM: sanctification of God's name
KIPA: skullcap
KIRUV: outreach
KLAL YISRAEL: the community of Israel
"KO SOMAR L'VAIS YAAKOV V'SAGID L'VNAI YIS-
    RAEL": "So you shall say to the House of Jacob
    and so you shall tell the children of Israel"
KOSHER: ritually acceptable
"LO SAAMOD AL DAM RAYECHA": "You shall not stand
    by idly while the blood of your friend is shed"
LOSHON HORA: evil speech
MAASER: tithe
MAYZID: deliberate offense
MEFORSHIM: commentaries
MEKAREV: bring close
MESORAH: tradition
MEZUZAH: portion of the Shema written on a scroll
    and placed on Jewish doorposts
MIDRASH: selection of rabbinic commentaries
MIKVAH: ritual bath
MINYAN: religious quorum required for public prayer
MITZVOS: commandments
NESHAMA: soul
NIDA: menstruating woman
PASUK: verse
PIRKEI AVOS: Ethics of the Fathers
OLAM HABAH: the World to Come
RAV: rabbi
RUCHNIUS: spirituality
SHABBOS: Sabbath

SHALOM BAYIS: marital harmony

SHMITTA: Sabbatical year

SHOGEG: accidental offense

SIYATA D'SHMAYA: Heavenly guidance

TEFILLIN: phylacteries

TOCHACHA: constructive criticism

TZADDIK: righteous person

TZITZIT: fringes placed on the corners of a four-corner
garment

"VE'AHAVTA L'RAYACHA KAMOCHA": "You shall love
your friend as yourself"

YETZER HARA: evil inclination

YETZER HATOV: good inclination

BIBLIOGRAPHY

Anyone interested in understanding and explaining Judaism should find the books and tapes listed here useful supplements to the information presented above. While many of these works are written for newcomers to Judaism, even individuals with a background in Jewish education will benefit from them, since they offer convenient and comprehensive coverage of topics whose treatment in original sources may span many dozens of volumes of Talmud and Midrash. Human oversight undoubtedly caused important and useful books to be omitted from this bibliography. We hope to rectify such lacunae in future editions, and we welcome any suggestions for additions to the bibliography.

OUTREACH/TESHUVA

Harris, Lis. HOLY DAYS: THE WORLD OF A HASIDIC FAMILY Summit 1985

Ms. Harris' portrayal of Orthodoxy, drawn from her year-long relationship with a Hasidic family in Brooklyn, is filled with good humor, respect, and surprisingly perceptive insights. Holy Days affords the religious reader a long look at himself through the eyes of a non-religious Jew.

Kelemen, Lawrence. PERMISSION TO BELIEVE Targum Press 1990

Four rational approaches to God's existence, particularly important for anyone involved in kiruv.

Kiel, Devora (ed.) RETURN TO THE SOURCE: SELECTED ARTICLES ON JUDAISM AND TESHUVA Feldheim 1984

This anthology, translated from the Hebrew original, contains numerous essays by Israeli educators and ba'alei teshuva. These include treatment of some of the issues and evidence discussed herein, as well as interesting personal accounts by Israelis from diverse backgrounds who returned to tradition.

Laufer, Mordechai (ed.) SEFER HASHLICHUT Kehot 1987

The obligation to engage in outreach, its benefits and methodology, are exhaustively examined in this 900 page Hebrew-language anthology.

Schiller, Mayer. THE ROAD BACK Feldheim 1989

A discovery and affirmation of authentic Judaism.

Schwartzbaum, Avraham. THE BAMBOO CRADLE Feldheim 1988

In this heartwarming and amusing nonfiction bestseller, a young Jewish academic and his wife adopt and raise a Chinese infant, and their desire to afford her a Jewish education eventually leads them to adopt a Torah lifestyle. Despite its uniqueness, their story is an excellent account of the intellectual and social processes experienced by many ba'alei teshuva.

Tatz, Akiva. ANATOMY OF A SEARCH Artscroll 1987

A South African surgeon traces his disaffection with Western secular society, and contrasts it with the advantages he found in the Orthodox way of life.

Willis, Ellen. "NEXT YEAR IN JERUSALEM" in Rolling Stone, April 1977

Ms. Willis' feature article about the experiences of her brother Michael (today, Rabbi Chaim) at Aish Ha-Torah is a pioneering classic in exploring the kiruv phenomenon.

PLURALISM

Aharoni-Fisch, R. Dov. JEWS FOR NOTHING Feldheim 1984

The outlook and motivations of those Jews who fall victim to the scourges of intermarriage, assimilation, and cults are analyzed here, and the insights gained will prove quite helpful in any contact with non-observant Jews.

Kahane, R. Meir. WHY BE JEWISH? Stein and Day 1977

In this powerful critique of the non-Orthodox movements, Rabbi Kahane presents a convincing case for laying the blame for rampant assimilation at the door of Reform, Conservative, and Reconstructionist Judaism. The author sharply illuminates the inconsistencies inherent in these brands of Judaism.

Packouz, R. Kalman. HOW TO STOP AN INTERMARRIAGE Aish HaTorah Publications 1976

A practical and effective guide to preventing tragedy for parents or friends of a potential partner in an intermarriage.

Safran, Eliyahu. CRISIS AND HOPE Esh Publications 1986

This slender volume traces the origins and influence of the Reform Movement; it will prove valuable to anyone desirous of understanding and combating the ongoing assimilation of American Jewry.

Schochet, R. Jacob Immanuel. WHO IS A JEW? Shofar 1987

Rabbi Schochet approaches this delicate topic with sensitivity and a rare calm rationality. This book directly addresses the Reform or Conservative Jew troubled by Orthodoxy's inability to accept their movements' conversions, and can serve as an excellent primer for religious Jews as well.

SCIENCE

Religious Perspective

The ranks of religious Jewry include outstanding scientists, many of whom have dedicated themselves to grappling with the issues raised by, and the alleged conflicts between, Torah and science. Unless otherwise noted, the volumes and journals listed here treat one or more of the common Torah/science questions, e.g., Genesis, the Big Bang, Evolution, etc.

Aviezer, Nathan. IN THE BEGINNING: BIBLICAL CREATION AND SCIENCE Ktav 1990

Branover, Herman. (ed.) "B'OR HATORAH" Shamir (multivolume)
Available in U.S., c/o Y. Hanoka 107 York Terrace Brookline MA 02146

Carmell, R. Aryeh and Domb, Cyril. CHALLENGE: TORAH VIEWS ON SCIENCE AND ITS PROBLEMS Feldheim 1978

Gotfryd, Arnie. (ed.) FUSION: ABSOLUTE STAND-ARDS IN A WORLD OF RELATIVITY Feldheim 1990

Levi, R. Leo. TORAH AND SCIENCE: THEIR INTER-PLAY IN THE WORLD SCHEME Feldheim 1983

"PROCEEDINGS OF THE ASSOCIATION OF ORTHO-DOX JEWISH SCIENTISTS" Feldheim 1969

Schimmel, R. H. Chaim and Carmell, R. Aryeh. EN-COUNTER: ESSAYS ON TORAH AND MODERN LIFE Feldheim 1989

Schroeder, Gerald. GENESIS AND THE BIG BANG Bantam 1990

Vitztum, Doron. HAMEIMAD HANOSAF Aguda Le-Mechkar Torani 1989

Dr. Vitztum is a pioneer in the novel field of computer search of the Torah text for equidistant letter skips — the so-called "codes". This Hebrew work is the first authorized publication explaining the methods and findings of these searches, and it contains fascinating examples of the statistically significant appearance of words "encoded" into the Torah.

Non-Religious Perspective

Denton, Michael. EVOLUTION: A THEORY IN CRISIS Burnett Books 1985

A thoroughly argued and documented survey of the current (as of 1985) state of the theory of evolution.

Hawking, Stephen W. A BRIEF HISTORY OF TIME Bantam 1988

Professor Hawking explores here the most current theories of the origins of the universe, and attempts, not always successfully, to convey them to the intelligent layman.

Hitchings, Francis. THE NECK OF THE GIRAFFE Pan Books 1982

Problems and weaknesses in the theory of evolution are examined here.

Hoyle, Fred and Wickramsinghe C. EVOLUTION FROM SPACE Dent 1981

Leading British scientist Sir Fred Hoyle and his colleague contend in this book that the initial stages of evolution, the generation of amino acids and DNA, are far too unlikely to have occurred by chance.

Jastrow, Robert. G-D AND THE ASTRONOMERS W.W. Norton 1978

Jastrow traces the evolution of cosmology, and the growing correspondence between the scientific and Biblical perspectives on the origin of the universe.

Weinberg, Steven. THE FIRST THREE MINUTES Basic Books 1988

This volume successfully achieves the goals set by *A Brief History of Time:* a comprehensive survey of the Big Bang and related theories for the origin of the universe.

TORAH AND COMMENTARIES

Hirsch, R. Samson Raphael. PENTATEUCH WITH HIRSCH COMMENTARY Judaica Press 1967

This classic commentary on the Chumash tackles many of the most relevant contemporary issues which arise in contacts with non-observant Jews.

Kaplan, R. Aryeh. THE LIVING TORAH Moznaim 1981

One of the most readable translations of the Torah, it includes study aids such as introduction, notes, maps, tables, charts, bibliography and index, which help bring the people and the events of Torah to life.

ANTI-SEMITISM

Religious Perspective

All of the Torah-oriented books below offer inspiring vignettes of spiritual fortitude in the face of the Nazi horror, as well as traditional Jewish perspectives on the Holocaust.

Allswang, Dr. Benzion. THE FINAL RESOLUTION: Combating Anti-Jewish Hostility Feldheim 1989

An analysis of how the abandonment of, rather than adherence to, Torah observance foments anti-Semitism.

Huberband, R. Shimon. KIDDUSH HASHEM: JEWISH RELIGIOUS AND CULTURAL LIFE IN POLAND DURING THE HOLOCAUST Ktav 1987

Prager, Moshe. SPARKS OF GLORY Artscroll 1985

A PATH THROUGH THE ASHES Artscroll 1986

THE UNCONQUERABLE SPIRIT Artscroll 1980

Non-Religious Perspective

Bat Yeor. THE DHIMMI: JEWS AND CHRISTIANS UNDER ISLAM Fairleigh Dickinson Univerity Press 1985

An excellent primer on the history of Muslim anti-Semitism, with many important implications for contemporary Arab hostility to Jews and Israel.

Dawidowicz, Lucy. THE WAR AGAINST THE JEWS Penguin 1977

The classic general history of the origins and development of the Nazi regime, and its policy towards the Jews. Required reading for anyone interested in the topic.

Flannery, Edward. THE ANGUISH OF THE JEWS MacMillan 1965

An excellent, comprehensive history of anti-Semitism, reaching from Greco-Roman times until the present day. Flannery is a Catholic priest, a fact which makes his unbiased account all the more shocking.

Gilbert, Martin. THE HOLOCAUST Holt 1985

Much more than just another study of the Holocaust, Gilbert infuses a chronological review of the dry facts with their full import and horror, through actual, vivid anecdotes from the Nazi inferno.

Hilberg, Raoul. THE DESTRUCTION OF THE EUROPEAN JEWS New Viewpoints 1973

Another classic, comprehensive review of the Nazi Holocaust.

Jackel, E. HITLER'S WORLDVIEW Harvard Press 1981

Hitler's anti-Jewish ideology parallels that of many of our enemies throughout history, and reveals a shocking familiarity with the traditional Jewish self-image, and a purposeful intent to undermine the Jews' quest to spread morality and monotheism. A grasp of this monstrous outlook can prove a useful tool for understanding the cyclical, dialectical patterns of Jewish history.

Mosse, George. THE CRISIS OF GERMAN IDEOLOGY Schocken 1981

(See comments to Jackel.)

Prager, Dennis and Telushkin, Joseph. ANTI-SEMITISM, WHY THE JEWS? Simon and Shuster 1980

An interesting study of the root causes of anti-Semitism.

Wistrich, Robert. HITLER'S APOCALYPSE: JEWS AND THE NAZI LEGACY Weidenfeld and Nicolson 1985

(See comments to Jackel.)

Wyman, David S. THE ABANDONMENT OF THE JEWS Pantheon 1984

This painful book examines the lack of Allied response to the slaughter of Jews during World War II.

GENERAL JEWISH PHILOSOPHY/HASHKAFA

Cardozo, R. Nathan T.L. THE INFINITE CHAIN Torah, Masorah and Man Targum Press 1989

An examination of the many facets of the Torah: the oral and written traditions and their relationship, Halachah and Aggadah.

Dessler, R. Eliyahu STRIVE FOR TRUTH (Edited and translated by R. Aryeh Carmell) Feldheim 1985, 3 vols.

This is the abridged, English version of Rabbi Dessler's classic Miktav M'Eliahu, which explores the conceptual underpinnings of virtually every Jewish ritual and idea.

Eisenberg, Rafael. SURVIVAL, ISRAEL AND MANKIND Feldheim 1991

By sublimating material goals into spiritual ones and applying the Torah to modern life, we prepare for Messianic peace.

Ellison, Getsel. SERVING THE CREATOR: A GUIDE TO THE RABBINIC SOURCES World Zionist Organization 1986

An educator will find this book, with its compilation of rabbinic sources on a topic by topic basis, an extremely useful tool for researching and teaching specific issues.

Fendel, R. Zechariah. CHALLENGE OF SINAI Rabbi Jacob Joseph School 1978

A series dealing with the conceptual and philosophical truths of Judaism, and the Torah approach to contemporary social challenges. Explores sexual mores, zero-population growth, abortion, drug culture, and intermarriage.

Gevirtz, R. Eliezer. L'HAVIN U'L'HASKIL: A GUIDE TO TORAH HASHKOFOH Feldheim 1980

Questions and answers about key issues in Jewish belief and practice, clearly organized by chapter.

Hirsch, R. Samson R.. COLLECTED WRITINGS Feldheim 1991 7 Vols.

All of Rabbi Hirsch's writings are useful and relevant, since he grappled in the 19th century with most of the issues which arise in contemporary contacts with non-observant Jews.

Hirsch, R. Samson R. HOREV (trans. and introduction by Dayan I. Grunfeld) Soncino 1962. See above

Hirsch, R. Samson R. NINETEEN LETTERS Feldheim 1969

Written in the format of a series of letters answering a student's inquiries on Torah, this work boldly answers the charge that Torah Judaism is old, decadent, and irrelevant.

Hurwitz, R. Shimon. BEING JEWISH Feldheim 1978

A critical analysis of Western society and values, contrasted with those proffered by the Torah.

Kaplan, R. Aryeh. IF YOU WERE GOD, National Conference of Synagogue Youth 1983

A slender work containing three sections: an essay on understanding God, by putting oneself in His role; a work on immortality and the soul; and "A World of Love", which deals with the purpose of creation.

Kaplan, R. Aryeh. HANDBOOK OF JEWISH THOUGHT Moznaim 1979

This is one of the most useful educational tools to appear in years. Rabbi Kaplan presents a highly systematic and thoroughly researched treatment of a broad range of theological issues.

Levi, Yehuda. TORAH STUDY: A Survey of Classic Sources on Timely Issues Feldheim 1990

This extensive collection addresses relevant issues, such as the conflict between Torah study and making a living.

Please feel free to call or write any of the Aish Ha-Torah branches for information on Kiruv programs or classes in your area. If there is no branch in your city, the Association of Jewish Outreach Professionals (212-221-2567) can assist you in finding the outreach program nearest you.

Aish HaTorah Cleveland
23112 Beachwood Blvd.
Cleveland, OH 44122
216-691-0859

Aish HaTorah Columbus
1989 Camaro Avenue,
Suite 210
Columbus, OH 43207
614-445-6800

Aish HaTorah Detroit
32712 Franklin Road
Franklin, MI 48025
313-737-0400

Aish HaTorah Jerusalem
P.O. Box 14149
Old City, Jerusalem, Israel
02-894-441

Aish HaTorah Los Angeles
9106 West Pico Boulevard
Los Angeles, CA 90035
310-278-8672

Aish HaTorah Miami
290 N.W. 165th Street
Miami, FL 33169
305-945-2155

**Aish HaTorah New York/
Discovery Seminars**
1388 Coney Island Avenue
Brooklyn, NY 11230
(718) 377-8819

Aish HaTorah St. Louis
8149 Delmar Avenue
St. Louis, MO 63130
314-862-2474

Aish HaTorah Toronto
296A Wilson Avenue
Downsview, Ontario M3H 1S8
416-636-7530

Aish HaTorah Washington
11617 Greenlane Drive
Potomac, MD 20854
301-983-1959

Appendix

AISH HATORAH'S
ONE-TO-ONE LEARNING PROGRAM

Aish HaTorah's New York branch sponsors a chavrusa learning program for students who desire the personal attention and tailored learning pace that a tutor can provide. The One-To-One Learning Program, held weekly in Manhattan and Brooklyn, pairs students of all interests and backgrounds with appropriately matched tutors, and offers participants the opportunity to study the subjects of their choice.

If you would like to volunteer as a tutor for this program or refer new students, please contact the Aish HaTorah office in New York, 1388 Coney Island Avenue, Brooklyn, NY 11230. (718-377-8819.)